How's it goin', boy?

How's it goin', boy?

Clíona O'Carroll
For The Northside Folklore Project

NONSUCH

Dedicated to all those who make Cork City what it is.
Keep on talking, keep on listening.

First published 2006

Nonsuch Publishing
73 Lower Leeson Street
Dublin 2
Ireland
www.nonsuchireland.com

British Library Cataloguing in Publication Data.
A catalogue record for this book is available from the British Library.

ISBN 1 84588 508 2
ISBN-13 (from January 2007) 978 1 84588 508 3

Typesetting and origination by Tempus Publishing Limited
Printed in Great Britain

Contents

Sponsors

THE NORTHSIDE FOLKLORE PROJECT

NORTHSIDE COMMUNITY ENTERPRISES LTD.
nce
Opening the Way
training - employment - enterprise

Cork 2005
European Capital of Culture
AIB
Official Partner

WHERE FINBARR TAUGHT LET MUNSTER LEARN

Cork 2005
European Capital of Culture
RTÉ   PREMIER PARTNER

Contributors

Here are the names and places of origin of the people whose interviews have been included in this book:

Karina Abdoulbaneeva, Russia

Dr. Mahbub Akhter, Bangladesh

Marcus Bale, Argentina

Alan Botan, Kurdistan, Northern Iraq

Brigid Carmody, Cork

Eileen Claffey, Co. Cork

Marie-Annick Desplanques, Brittany, France

Geoffrey D'Souza, India

Robert Fourie, South Africa

Noreen Geaney, Co. Cork

Noreen Hanover, Cork

Andy Hawkins, Cork

Ge Hei, China

Tony Henderson, Canada

Emeka Ikebuasi, Nigeria

Dearbhla Kelleher, Cork

Vitaliy Mahknanov, Ukraine

Patrícia Manresa, Spain

Billy McCarthy, Cork

Tim O'Brien, Cork

Kay O'Carroll, Cork

B.O'D., Slovakia

Michael O'Flynn, Cork

Mícheál Ó Geallabháin, Cork

Mary O'Sullivan, Cork

Avreimi Rot, Israel

Aimée Setter, England

Isabelle Sheridan, France

Adam Skotarczak, Poland

Rob Stafford, Australia

Liz Steiner-Scott, USA

Yossi Valdman, Israel

Lode Vermeulen, The Netherlands

Stephen Wimpenny, England

Stefan Wulff, Germany

Lily Xiong, China

Acknowledgements

The Northside Folklore Project would like to thank all of our ongoing sponsors: Northside Community Enterprises, Ltd; FÁS; Roinn an Bhéaloidis/Department of Folklore & Ethnology, UCC. We must also thank Cork 2005, who provided funding for the original project that this book is based around. Special thanks to Gearóid Ó Crualaoich, Roinn an Bhéaloidis, for the long-term support and inspiration in the area of community folklore.

The people who put the book together:
Editor and NFP Cork 2005 Special Project Coordinator: Dr. Clíona O'Carroll
NFP Project Manager and Assistant Editor: Mary O'Driscoll
NFP Research Director: Dr. Marie-Annick Desplanques
Photographic Research: Fawn Allen; Maureen O'Keefe
Additional Photography: Fawn Allen
Research: Breda Sheehan; Shane Walsh
Technical Assistance: Colin MacHale
Interview Transcription: Sean Claffey; Breda Sheehan
Proofreading: Máire O'Carroll

Interviews conducted by: Jennifer Butler; Lee Cassidy; Sean Claffey; Dianne Hoppe; Dolores Horgan; John Mehegan; Cliona O'Carroll; Mary O'Driscoll; Noel O'Shaughnessy; Frances Quirke

Thanks also to Michael Lenihan and Tom Foley for their time and assistance with photographs.

Photographic Acknowledgements

The photographs in this book were taken by various Northside Folklore Project staff or came from the family and personal collections of the contributors. Thanks to all contributors for trusting us with their photos.

Cover photographs: Fawn Allen. See the centre colour section for cover photo captions.

Page 103 and 124 Finbarr O'Regan

The chief NFP photographer, Fawn Allen, took the following photographs:
Ch 2: pages 27 (bottom), 29, 31 (all)
Ch 3: page 42
Ch 4: page 52
Ch 6: page 66
Ch 7: page 71
Ch 9: pages 84, 85
Ch 11: pages 96 (all) 97, 100, 101,104, 106 (all), 107,108,110,111
Ch 13: page 119
Ch 14: page 128

Colour section:
Numbers: 1, 3, 4, 8, 9, 10, 11, 15, 18, 19 20, 21, 23, 24, 25, 26, 27, 28, 30, 32, 33

How's it goin', boy? Radio Series

This book is a companion volume to a series of six half-hour radio programmes of the same name, produced as part of Cork 2005, European Capital of Culture. A box set of the programmes is available from the Northside Folklore Project.
NFP website: http://www.ucc.ie/research/nfp

Northside Folklore Project
Northside Community Enterprises Ltd.
Sunbeam Industrial Park
Mallow Road
Cork

About the Editor

Clíona O'Carroll teaches with Roinn an Bhéaloidis/Department of Folklore and Ethnology, University College, Cork. An interviewer, radio producer and ethnographic fieldwork trainer, she was special project co-ordinator for the Cultures of Cork project for which these interviews were carried out, and produced the resulting series of six radio programmes. She lives in Cork, just off the Fever Hospital Steps.

Foreword from the Project Manager

2005 and Cork's year as 'European Capital of Culture' was in many ways a turning point for the Northside Folklore Project. Creating first the radio series and then the book of *How's it goin', boy?* has resulted in a wide range of long term benefits for the project and our FÁS staff. Extensive training, new equipment and software have grown our capabilities. The challenging and stimulating process of conducting the interviews proved to be a wonderful and extremely satisfying team building experience, broadening our horizons and world views. The source material collected adds an exciting new multi-cultural dimension to our permanent archive. The contacts and friends made are the foundation of a valuable network for the future and are an aspect of our newly heightened profile in the community. For us, Cork 2005 was all good.

There are two other people who need special thanks, first, the dedicated big thinker, Marie-Annick Desplanques, without whom the Northside Folklore Project would simply not exist, and Clíona O'Carroll, for her enthusiasm, knowledge, patience and determination. It was a joy working with you.

Oh, and by the way, I'm American by birth, and Corkonian by choice.

Mary O'Driscoll
Project Manager
Northside Folklore Project

Research Director's Note

The Northside Folklore Project (NFP) is a multimedia research and community archive documenting traditional and popular culture, and the local and oral history of Cork city. Based on the Northside of the city, its innovative structure is comprised of a tri-lateral partnership between the department of Folklore and Ethnology at University College Cork (UCC), Northside Community Enterprises (NCE) at the local level and FÁS, the national training and employment authority. It was created in 1996 as a result of significant developments in the research programme in Folklore and Ethnology at UCC, which also involved the establishment of a Folklore and Ethnology Archive at the University in 1995. By creating an important educational and cultural resource while providing community-based employment, NFP brings a social and economic dimension into its cultural framework. Through its intellectual premises and methodologies it operates within the discipline of Folklore and Ethnology, whose academic ethos incorporates a humanities dimension through a social science perspective; this particularly and pragmatically implies an insider-outsider approach to the ethnographic fieldwork and collection projects its researchers carry out.

The Project simultaneously promotes academic research and community development. Its archived multimedia collection of over 10,000 photographs, 600 hours of audio and 150 hours of video-recorded ethnographic and oral history material is the result of the work of an integrated team of community researchers, postgraduate students and academics. The research agenda emerges from factors linked to community interest and funding programmes, support having come from academic, state and government bodies, as well as from the private sector.

Over the past ten years NFP received Higher Education Authority (HEA) funding which has assisted in the digitisation of its collection to eventually produce part of a multidisciplinary integrated database known as *Documents of Ireland*. Other academic funding and opportunities at UCC and from government programmes, particularly those sponsoring students' internships, allowed for the creation of a portable exhibition, the publication of the book, *Life Journeys,* and the creation of a multimedia website. Such funding also enables the NFP to publish its annual journal *The Archive,* which is distributed free of charge in Cork city and digitally made available through the website. Links forged in the community have led to a network which has enabled NFP to receive expertise in the production of audio and video programming, and more importantly to establish credibility among the community of people who have contributed their knowledge to the NFP archive and to further its reputation in Cork city and well beyond.

During Cork's year as European Capital of Culture, NFP's archive and research resources contributed to several other programmes and projects for Cork 2005. Most significantly NFP obtained funding for the major ethnographic project that created the radio series, *How's it goin', boy?* and eventually led to the production of this book.

Dr. Marie-Annick Desplanques,
NFP Research Director,
Department of Folklore and Ethnology,
University College Cork.

Introduction

Who are the people of Cork city; what are the memories, stories and meanings associated with the spaces they move through and the people they meet? What is the 'everyday' of the city? When the call went out for project ideas for the celebration of Cork's tenure as European Capital of Culture, the Northside Folklore Project rose to the occasion. As a community-based folklore collection and archiving project, we were particularly interested in representing the 'everyday' of the City of Culture.

We carried out an ethnographic project to explore a slice of everyday life in the city through more than forty interviews with people from all walks of life. The interviews were deposited in our archive, and we created a series of six radio programmes from the material. This book is another opportunity to share some of the memories, stories and experiences that came out of the encounter.

Listening to the interviews or reading the transcriptions, the first thing that strikes you is the range of experiences represented. We wanted to reflect the increase in the mix of national backgrounds in the city by seeking out people who had come to Cork from elsewhere as well as those born and bred in the city. There was also a wide range in age, in occupations, and in religious and ethnic backgrounds. The unifying factor is the way in which each person has a particular and intimate relationship with the city: what emerges is the flavour of Cork as observed, experienced and engaged with by the diverse bunch of people sharing its space. For Billy McCarthy, the Lough holds the memory of him falling in with his brother's bike over forty years ago; for Dr. Mahbub Akhter it conjures up the image of his first jet-lagged city walk after a sixteen-hour journey from Bangladesh. The surprising meaning of the phrase 'how bad' is decoded and celebrated by a Slovakian woman, while Patrícia Manresa from Spain and Mary O'Sullivan from Ballyphehane both know not to hold their breath when a request to a family member is answered with 'I will, yeah.'

There's more movement in the world than ever before. The everyday of Cork is changing through this, with a confluence of so many different worlds on the streets of the city.

When people hear the word 'folklore', they think of a shared past. There's no one single shared past in this city, but we certainly have a shared present. The aim of this project was to take a snapshot of that present, and all the diverse memories and experiences supporting it, to put it out there and say: 'This is who we are right now.'

We started the project by preparing interviews and developing questions. We wanted to develop an understanding of 'the interview' as a series of cycles of memory with varying intensity; as an interaction between two people; as a series of branching pathways of enquiry rather than a two-dimensional list of questions to be posed. What areas of enquiry to follow was a key consideration: it's impossible to discuss someone's entire life in an hour or two, and we favoured richness of description and fondly-held memories over volumes of information. Although we wanted to look at the city as it is now, we recognised that the contemporary everyday is underlayed with our memories and pasts: the neighbourhoods, far and near, that we grew up in; our elders; the games we played; the food we ate; and the places we loved.

We decided to look at the following areas in depth with all interviewees:

Their childhood neighbourhoods and lives, special places and elders, their current relationship with the city and everyday routine, favourite places, and observations on change in Cork.

For those who had come to Cork from elsewhere, there were some extra themes to explore:

First impressions of Cork, stories from their early days in the city, including misunderstandings and difficulties, and the process of adjustment to different ways of thinking, speaking and, sometimes, being.

We also prepared some set-phrase questions for everyone: for example they were invited to talk about phrases that they associate with Cork, talk about three words that describe the city for them, and give a message for the people of Cork.

After all our preparations with questions and equipment, a high point came when we started doing interviews, and the interviewees stopped being an abstract, unknown, and turned into living, breathing people who welcomed us into their homes and their lives with an openness that overwhelmed us. Being an interviewer can be challenging and scary, and the potential lack of a shared background had also prompted some worries about interviewing 'strangers': What if we can't understand each other because of accent or language differences? What if I say something wrong, or insulting, or too personal, but don't realise it because of a cultural gap? These preoccupations receeded as the project gained momentum. The personal contact with so many new people, the insights into their generously shared lives, and all that we learned through it, was exhilirating and hugely enriching.

Then, at our weekly planning meeting, as we discussed what themes were emerging for the radio programmes, people would come back from interviews, or from listening to each others' interviews, filled up with stories. We would sit, eight or nine interviewers, around a big table and one story or comment from one interview would start us talking about something similar in another, in turn sparking off memories or observations from our own lives. And so it would go, round and round. *Beireann sceal sceal eile*: one story gives birth to another. After a while it felt as if all the interviewees were there as well. And sometimes some of their parents, grandparents, favourite uncles, first loves…

The material generated from the interviews was rich and plentiful. Unfortunately, this very fact posed a problem for us when editing the radio programmes: we simply had too much good stuff. It was a pleasure, therefore, to return to the material for this book, and to have a chance to let more of these voices and stories be heard in printed form, along with some illustration from family photographs. We organised the book into two kinds of chapters and alternated them: some chapters follow a theme, while others follow one person's voice. Inevitably, the old problem soon reemerged. For every story, memory and image in this book there are many more in each interview just as deserving of being shared, and tough choices had to be made in deciding what to leave out.

Any such project is very much a team affair, with a lot of hard work shared between a number of people. At the start of the process the NFP team jumped into the unknown with enthusiasm, hard work, openness and inspiration. Interviewing, technically processing and transcribing the interviews, liaising with contributors about photographs, scanning and processing the photographs, checking details and place names: these are all fields in which Fawn Allen, Jenny Butler, Lee Cassidy, Sean Claffey, Dianne Hoppe, Dolores Horgan, Colin McHale, John Mehegan, Mary O'Driscoll, Maureen O'Keefe, Noel O'Shaughnessy, Breda Sheehan, Frances Quirke and Shane Walsh invested a lot of time and effort and at which they excelled. Thanks to all for the sustained, patient and cheerful effort that saw this book to completion. The Project Manager and Assistant Editor Mary O'Driscoll was, as ever, an organisational lynchpin and a well of support, fresh ideas, good humour, wit and warmth.

At the Northside Folklore Project, we transcribe every single interview, writing it out word for word. It can take eight hours of transcription per hour of conversation, and so the transcription of forty-two interviews averaging about an hour each was a mammoth job. The transcription staff, Sean Claffey and Breda Sheehan, carried out trojan work.

Most of all we would like to thank the contributors to this book - the interviewees. When someone asks you to be interviewed about, 'Well, no particular topic, just, y'know, everyday life,' it takes a generous person to say yes. It took even more generosity to share such warmth, memories, emotions, humour, and so much of themselves, as they did. Thank you.

Writing conversation: transcription and editing

Two truths are inescapable when you want to represent conversations or interviews in a book:

1. You lose a lot when you put the spoken word on the page - laughter, accents, warmth, emphasis, humour, timing and delivery.

2. Because of the difference between what we expect from the written word and what we accept as normal for the spoken word, the way we speak rarely looks good when you put it down on paper.

Some of the immediacy of the occasion and the expressiveness of the delivery is inevitably lost through the process of committing the spoken word to print. Turning transcribed words into edited exerpts for the book is a process that moves the material yet another step from the original interaction. Normal conversation is often littered with unfinished sentences and incoherent grammatical structures. The spoken word is not comfortable to read when it is transcribed exactly and the fact that English is not the first language of many of the contributors meant that some formulations appear incongruous on paper. The editing of this book involved punctuating and manipulating the transcription to make them more print-friendly. However, we remained as close as possible to what was said, and tried to be consistent with the editing process. We outline below some of the ways that we dealt with this, stressing that any mistakes in the final text are ours.

We edited out false starts, repetition, hesitations, digressions, and phrases such as 'd'you know.' Many contributors' speech was punctuated by Cork phrases, such as 'like.' We left some in, but in the interests of readability hundreds and hundreds of 'like's were cut out, from native Cork people and newer Corkonians alike. In order to keep the flavour of the spoken word, non-standard grammar was usually left unchanged, particularly with local Cork usages, such as saying 'we used' instead of 'we used to.' In the case of those whose first language isn't English, we sometimes inserted or deleted the articles 'a' and 'the' and changed verb tenses in order to make the text easier to read. Any other text inserted by us and not spoken by the contributor is enclosed in [square brackets]. We used *italics* to show when a word was emphasised. We used … to indicate where we have taken out some text or where the contributor paused significantly or changed track.

Our decision not to include our questions in the text does mask the context of the statements, or the reason why a person is talking about a particular theme. However, we felt that the book would flow better if the interviewers' questions were omitted.

A request to the reader
Any interview is an interaction of the moment. It represents what comes into a person's head (and out of their mouths) on a particular day, in a particular place, in conversation with a particular person and in response to particular questions or probes. The exerpts in this book represent slices of conversations, sometimes taken out of their context and rearranged, and are not something that the contributor has carefully formulated in order to represent their lives. We hope that the reader will bear this in mind, and will enter into the conversation as a witness to life in Cork as expressed 'in the moment.'

Some of the interviewees were found through word of mouth, others through different organisations in Cork. None were chosen for being 'expert' at anything but everyday life. In a way, the best thing Cork 2005 gave us was an excuse to ask about the ordinary, with extraordinary results. We hope this book will bring out the memories and experiences that resonate with readers - the things we share - and open up a window on the things that are new to us, a passing glimpse of other lives: lives outside of our experience, but part of our shared present.

Clíona O'Carroll
How's it goin', boy? Project Co-ordinator and Editor

1

Neighbourhoods

We've all ended up in Cork: here's a taste of where some of us started out. City, country, suburbia: the neighbourhoods we come from vary, but for each of us they're the scene and setting of our early memories.

Andy Hawkins

I was born in the Marsh and I spent my first seven years in the Marsh. I started school at four like most kids of that era, St. Francis' School. My father had a little business at the time, a carpentry workshop in the Marsh. I don't remember much about him because he died when I was young. One happy memory I have of the Marsh is a man called John Walsh. In them days he used to sell what we used to call 'little sticks,' bundles of sticks. People used to buy these little bundles of sticks to light the fire, and once a week he'd come around to the Marsh and he'd always put me up on the donkey and give me a lift on the donkey from one end of the street to the other.

Eileen Claffey

I grew up on a farm in West Cork. I lived with my mother and father, and one brother and four sisters. We had no electricity, we used to have oil lamps and open fires. I remember the first radio we got … My father was very quiet but rather strict. He was hard-working, also my mother was a very hard-working person. She used to work twelve hours or more a day, tending to the farm animals, and doing the housework inside as well as outside, and she would help neighbours as well. We would bring in the cows and help my parents with the milking, and we used to separate the cream from the milk, and sometimes we used to drink the cream. It used to be lovely. My sister and myself, we'd bring the cows home for milking, and take them out again, and feed the chickens, and the ducks and pigs. We all had our different jobs to do, and then in the afternoon we'd play for a while. We used to play football in school, the boys against the girls.

Late May, June, we used to save the hay. Then August, September, the corn: I used to bind sheaves of corn. From late September to November we would be bringing in the harvest, bringing in the potatoes and the vegetables. We used to pick the potatoes. I remember it used to be very cold. In the summertime we had quite a lot to do outside. We preferred being outside than doing jobs inside. I didn't like doing housework. I didn't like doing the washing up, I tried to get out of it.

Left: Rob Stafford and a tinglewood tree, a type of tree similar to the karri tree, Western Australia.

Opposite: Dearbhla Kelleher, Bonfire Night 1999. Dearbhla is in the centre.

Rob Stafford

I remember when I was very small we had a 200-acre farm, way down the south west of Western Australia. And they have these karri trees, they're one of the biggest trees in the world, eucalyptus trees. A lot of the pioneers, what they did to kill them was ring-barked them so they died ... so you have these fields full of skeleton karri trees, and the light could go in, and they just ploughed and planted around them. So we had this 200 acres, and gradually, one by one, my father was cutting them down, and as you can imagine these trees would be about three metres diameter ... and I remember he cut one of these trees down and I was standing about thirty, forty metres away, and the tree fell and the whole ground shook. I remember that all right, that was quite exciting.

Dearbhla Kelleher

I grew up in Ballyvolane, up in the Northside of Cork city, and I'm there all my life so far. It's off the main road so it's fairly quiet all right, like. There's kind of a square in our park and everybody used to meet there every summer, and we used to play games like rounders, and there was release and tip the can. I remember tip the can and just chasing, and things like that, do you know, hopscotch. It was a good laugh all right. Even the bigger children, they'd be older now than us, they'd be joining in with the smaller ones.

I'd have only been maybe about five or six at the time, but we'd have good summers, we'd have a good time all right.

The only thing I miss about the park is the stream down there. Falling into the stream down there, coming home - my mam would kill me: 'Did you get wet again?' We used to have little camps over the wall there, kind of a big wall at the end of our park and it was, like, forbidden to go past the wall because it was so wet and marshy and, oh, there was everything … It was a health hazard, like, but sure what harm. We had a brilliant time in the stream, down the tunnels down the end of the park as well. We used to sit under there and everything. I mean the crawling things there … I'd say the dirt was unreal, but sure we didn't know the difference. [There] was kinda like … piping going across the stream, you'd be trying to get across but sure if you lost your balance you were gone. Come home: 'Did you fall in the stream?' 'No.' And they dug that all up, it's all covered, so no more stream.

Ge Hei

In China we do not have a lot of houses like here. We have apartments, so on one floor we have five or six neighbours. The people are not very rich but that's OK: they help each other. For example, if today in my house we're short rice or something, or it's hard to get, maybe my neighbour knows that and then they just give us some and they say, 'OK, it's no problem.' So we just help each other very often. I have good memories from when I was child because I think our neighbourhood is very nice and friendly.

Michael O'Flynn
I was born on the Southside, and I lived all my life in Turner's Cross, Derrynane Road, before I got married and moved to the South Douglas Road. All my family live in Turner's Cross and the surrounding area. I went to Sullivan's Quay school. Back in the late 50s when we played soccer, you could actually be suspended from your school because of the ban – they wanted you to play GAA with the school, but we played soccer because all my friends were going to Turner's Cross we all played for our local team.

My father worked in Eustaces before it closed down, and he went to Hartes, he worked in Hartes, he drove a lorry for H. Harte & Co. and worked very, very hard. He would bring loads of timber all over County Cork, and when the ship, when the timber came in that time at night, into the quay side, he might have to work all night drawing - as he said himself - drawing the timber from the boat up to what they called their storage yard up in Clark's Quay. It's no longer there now, there's apartments and houses built there now.

Robert Fourie
I'm from the Republic of South Africa. I was born there in 1969, in the little city called Welkom, which is a gold mining city in the goldfields project in the Free State Province. The Free State Province is a maize province, parts of it are semi-desert, and it's quite a dry area. There's not much water there - there's no river running through the city - and it's a very flat town with only a little hill on the horizon, and that's the only landmark feature that you can see, otherwise it is completely flat - very good for cycling. The people there are mostly Sutu speakers, which is an African language. There are a lot of Afrikaans-speaking people, who originate from the Dutch people who arrived in South Africa, and there are some English-speaking people in Welkom, and I'm from a minority of English-speaking South Africans who live in that city.

The city is very dry, I'd nearly say semi-desert, and thorn bush kind of thing. It's very inland, very flat, very dusty, and in August we have a lot of wind. The sky would become red at times with dust, and very dark sometimes, and you would have to go indoors because the wind would be blowing so badly. Sometimes a joke would be made, 'Oh, look, there comes the next town,' the town down the road, over with the wind, because all the farmers' land would be blowing over the city. There are very often droughts where we would have water restrictions, we would only have drinking water, we all had to share the bath water at home, and not flush the loos and that kind of thing. There would be times when there would be a great shortage of water, and so people have quite an awareness of saving water and being careful with water, and the preciousness of water.

None of my direct family are gold miners, but my brother-in-law was a gold miner and he used to tell some very interesting stories about going down underneath in the mines and how a lot of the indigenous local people who work in the mines have beliefs about ghosts of people who died in the mines. There is a lot of what the Irish would call *piseogs*. Another story that he told us about was, people get depressed working under the mines

Robert Fourie and his sister sitting on tree stump in their front garden in Welcom.

– you know the difficulties of life being migrant workers – a lot of these men who would be working underground would eventually get depressed and commit suicide by jumping down a mine shaft. One thing he told us was that people jumping down a mine shaft, when they were going to commit suicide, they take their clothes off, their boots off, and they fold everything neatly and they jump down the shafts naked … Stories as well that would frighten me, you would have forty people in a lift going down in the mine and sometimes you know the metal rope would go slack, and then you would be free-falling down this hole in a lift and it would be really frightening for the miners. There are a lot of stories and traditions of things that happen underneath the ground … there is a very rich kind of story life in the mines in South Africa.

The migrant workers would have their own chants and songs that they would bring from their own [home places], like Malawi would be a country north of South Africa, and Mozambique, a lot of those people would bring chants and songs, they would be in a language that we wouldn't understand. One of the things in South Africa is that we have so many different languages and so many different cultures, that you would generally at least know two languages in South Africa very, very fluently, and many black people in South Africa can speak more than three or four languages very fluently, so the typical city worker in Johannesburg might be able to speak English, Afrikaans, Zulu and Sutu, and then maybe another language. There are very rich differences in culture, and people are quite aware of them.

Tim O'Brien
Well, I was born in the Backwatercourse Road, just off the Fever Hospital steps. Pope's Road was the road going up the side of the house. In the front you had Watercourse

Road, which was the main route for all the water that was flowing down from Blackpool. The Glen, I saw that being opened up and I saw a little train inside there doing repair works. I was living directly besides Murphy's brewery: my father worked in Murphy's brewery, so that was probably why we lived there. Behind us then we had what was called the plots, and Roche's Buildings were behind that, so we used to play up and down there. We did all the things that kids still do to this day. There were a couple of orchards around the place and we used to visit them occasionally. We used to be chased, just the same as everyone else.

My father worked in Murphy's Brewery for forty-two years. He was the third generation of his family that worked there, and at the time it was reckoned to be a good job – once you got into it you were there for life. But they used to live, eat, and breathe their job. If you worked for Murphy's Brewery you couldn't drink the product that was made by anyone else, or you'd lose your job. I remember the last two horses they had there before they went over to trucks, big grey horses, shire-horses, massive things altogether, and their stables there were in what was called the 'bottling sort,' it's a car park now. Two big huge horses, and then there was only one and then obviously there was none, and 'tis all trucks now. But it was nice to see the horses moving up and down Blackpool, pulling their barrels up and down to the pubs. And the women used to be out with their bags and their shovels to collect the droppings from the horse for the gardens, for the roses, that was a bit of a treasure as well if you got it. But some things that were old are gone; you'll never see the likes of it again.

Behind our houses then there was a thing called the Fever Hospital, and that was just a place that you were afraid of for some reason, we didn't know why. The people in the area were afraid of it, and that fear communicated itself on down the generations down to us, and we were afraid of it too, but we never knew what we were afraid of. Of course, when we got to ten or twelve we used to climb over the wall and go in and have a look around and get chased out of it, like. Later on we found out we were talking about polio, but when we were growing up we had no idea of what we were talking about. It was just the fever hospital, a place to run away from, you know . . .

Mahbub Akhter
I'm from Bangladesh, and my home city is called Rãjshãhi, it's to the north side of Bangladesh, very close to India. My dad works in a university, and my mum was a schoolteacher, she retired three years ago. From my childhood, I always wanted to be a good sportsman so I used to play a lot everywhere, most of my spare time I used to play different sports, and my parents, they didn't like it too much, because we are mainly the typical middle class, you know, where education is best for you, sports, that means you're spoilt or something.

I had quite a few good friends there, we grew up together; we used to play together, and we used to go to school together. It was a very quiet place, although it's very busy these days. If I go home nowadays I can hardly recognise the place. It's more populated, because near my house we could see the paddy fields. It was the mid seventies ... we had hardly any toys. I remember I had a small tricycle, and I was so proud of it. It was a not so busy street, there were a few fields besides the street, it was very quiet, it's more like a park than a street. It looked quite green, and one or two rickshaw, or maybe bicycle. Sometimes we used to play a local game called carom. The carom, it's a sort of billiard, circular flat, like the ice hockey puck. It's an indoor game.

Patrícia Manresa

My home-town is called Tortosa, it's a hundred miles south of Barcelona. It's quite a big town – there are 40,000 people living there. It has grown a lot in recent years; it used to be quite small and unimportant when I was small. But tourism is developing in the area, so that's why it's becoming bigger and bigger. Well, my mother being Irish, she couldn't see herself living in a flat in town. Like in the town, people just live in flats, I suppose Spain is mainly flats. She always lived in a house and she thought the idea of living in a flat was very claustrophobic. My parents moved outside the town, and into a very small house where it didn't even have water or electricity. Nobody lived around in the outskirts of the city at that time - there were only small houses where farmers used to keep all their stuff, like, for farming. So they moved into that house, and originally it was the only house in the area, but bit by bit people started to build on the outskirts of the city, so at one stage my house was very isolated, but now it's surrounded by loads of houses.

Bit by bit I got to know the neighbours. My closest neighbour was a farmer, and he would show me all the techniques in the area, how to get the water. Of course, Spain is a dry country, so he'd have to dig the ground, and make kind of channels so the water could go from tree to tree. And I remember the orange trees, and the lemon trees, and especially the olive trees.

Looking back now, what I miss most of Spain would be the smell of the country. It's quite different to Ireland, and I suppose I only got to appreciate what I had when I came to Ireland, or when I was living in Barcelona, a city where you don't have the silence of the country. Silence to me, to be able to withdraw from everything and have my own space and my own time, is very important.

My favourite place as a child

I used to walk to school every day, and I would find my own shortcuts to get down to school. And there was this small shortcut that went from my house to my neighbour's house, and I just had to climb down walls and go through the fields. There was special spot where there was a huge olive tree and there was a broken-down wall, and every time I went down to school I used to stop there for five minutes and just look at the view of the town from that place. And it was the only place in the whole shortcut that there was green grass - it wasn't rocky like on the rest of the walk - and there were flowers as well in the spring time, [in] that special spot that I had, and that's the place that I enjoyed being most when I was small.

2

Noreen Hanover

I grew up in Nicholas Church Place, it's just off Cove Street, Evergreen Street area. Well when I grew up it was in the fifties, our house was a tenement house, a few of the neighbours had top and bottom houses, upstairs and downstairs, but we didn't have. We kind of envied them really, our friends and our neighbours like that. It was a grand area to live in.

Everything was in Barrack Street, there were lots of old pubs and small grocery shops, and right on top of our own street, Nicholas Church Street, there was a shop; Mrs. Murphy used to own it. My mother used to shop there for food, a pound of butter, or two pound of sugar and four or five dozen of eggs, or whatever, and she'd write them down at the end of the week. My mother used to work then, after my dad died. Myself and Rose were the bigger ones, and we'd go up and get things, and my mother used to kill us at the end of the week - we were getting all the things we weren't supposed to get, maybe a quarter pound of biscuits or an extra pound of butter, and she'd be saying, 'What were ye doing with the butter at all?' She'd kill you over the butter and that, like.

I suppose our games were seasonal games – picky, skipping, or release, jumping the steps. Where we were living there were steps like, once I jumped the whole ten steps . . . If we were playing release, now, we could go off to Evergreen Street or up Friar Street or down onto the Grand Parade, or all around the area like that for playing games. Release would be one game. Boys and girls [would play] but you'd be all embarrassed then if your mother saw you being caught by a boy, you know. He'd bring you back to the den, you'd be caught by the elbow in case you'd run away, and your mother would be at the door, and you'd be given out to, and you'd be all embarrassed with the boys being around. And getting back to games of the house now, we nearly all had a doll. We'd get a toy for Christmas, so like, during the summer the doll would be broken. We'd make a paper doll with newspaper. I often made a doll a foot long with newspaper, and if you got brown paper it was a great novelty, because you could draw a face with the brown paper, whereas with the newspaper she'd have no face. There was a woman living near us who was a dressmaker, and we used to have her scourged for old rags and bits of trimmings off the things that she'd have, and you'd make clothes and scarves for the doll, and we'd dress her up, and you'd be there for all hours of the morning, playing away.

Right: Nicholas Church Place: the view looking downhill from the house that Noreen's family and another family shared.

Below: Barrack Street, 2006.

There must be thousands of photographs of us somewhere in America. Where we were living in Nicholas Church Place there's a Protestant Church, and the Americans would be coming, tourists, and they'd be up at the Church, and they'd see all us kids playing games and they'd be all around you, taking pictures of you, and lining ye on the steps and asking your names: there were thousands of pictures taken of us.

The older sister, Rose, is three years older than me, and, like, she played with you up to a certain age, but then when she got twelve, thirteen and that, she got notions about boys, so you weren't wanted then no more, and they'd go off to Greenmount and Crosses Green sussing out fellas and that like, and we had our own games.

We were living in a tenement house, and we had two bedrooms on one side. There was no actual door hanging, there was a doorframe to go from one bedroom to the other, and the thing for the latch in the door would be still there, and hinges would be still there. And we'd get a rope or a hard piece of twine and put a pillow on it or a coat, and we'd play swings, and that was our indoor swing, our own playground like, having fun that way.

In our street alone there was seven houses and there were fifty kids, there was seven or eight in ours, like. My mother was a great storyteller, and the four steps then, it was always known as the four steps … It might be half past ten, [in] summer you would be finished playing the games, it was just starting to get dark, and someone would say, 'Mrs Walsh, will you tell us stories?' And she might tell one or two stories and, sure, all the kids would be after gathering, and next thing someone would say, 'I'm going up home to get a coat to sit on.' So she'd say, 'OK, everybody, get what you're getting.' You might get a jumper or a cardigan or a coat, or an old blanket, and the children used to be [there], and she used to be sitting in the middle of all them, telling them ghost stories.

Noreen's family and the family that shared the house with them at the beach.

'The Four Steps', 2006.

She would be telling us all about the headless coaches up across Fort Street, up off Barrack Street. It was kind of well known, it would be an area now you wouldn't go much because it was always known for ghosts and banshees and all those kind of things, like. The banshee was another great one like, that was supposed to be a woman with long hair and a veil. My mother would used to be telling stories about people dying, and they'd say they'd hear the rattles of death. I don't know are there any rattles of death like, sure people do that when they're going to die anyway, because they're breaking up, but she'd be telling it in a way that they'd hear the rattles of death. That's the way our summer nights used to end.

On a Saturday night we'd have a bath. She had a big huge galvanised bath out in the back yard. And me father would say, 'Time for me to go now,' and he'd bring in the bath, and he'd go off to the pub then and she'd bath us. And one by one then, like, in line you were washed, and you were shivering then, and put in by the fire, and there was a stool in the corner, it was the nearest spot to the fire, so you were put directly into the corner. And then the next fella came out and you were moved accordingly around the fire. And she'd have on a bit of ham or a bit of bacon, or maybe a couple of crubeens −they were a famous food in Cork, like, pig's feet. And she had a couple of them for me Dad when he'd come in from the pub, but there was a lovely smell from it. We used to be going in and out with slices of bread, dipping bread into the water that it was being boiled in, and you might go through a whole sliced pan between the four of us. You might spend the rest of the night up, gasping, looking for water then all night, because you'd be after having so many dips, like.

We would be allowed go up the baths in the summer time and there was an outdoor pool, which Cork doesn't have now like, and we would go up there. We didn't have swimming suits, let me tell you, it would be in our old underwear. That's what all the girls used to have, it was our old knicks [knickers] we used to have, navy knicks. We would have to walk all the way up the Lee Fields, it seemed like miles when I look back on it, and coming back you'd always be trying to make shortcuts. We might come across College Road, down Magazine Road, and you'd come onto Gilabbey Street, and where St. Fin Barre's Cathedral is, the back road to that. You'd come out onto the top of Barrack Street, along onto Fort Street, and there are two angels in the structure of the Church, and we'd make a *run* across there from one end of Fort Street, we'd run from one end to the other, because the story always had it, at the end of the world it was those two angels that would blow the trumpets. And we would be petrified that she would blow the trumpet when we were passing, so you'd make a run across it and even if you were gone past it and she blew it, at least you were nearer home. And you'd still do it the next time, just to get a shortcut home.

Changes and memories
[Moving to Ballyvolane] was a vast change, I was moving from the Southside to the Northside, and my husband was also from the Southside. It was a big change to us, but the very fact of having a house was fantastic after living in a tenement house all my life. [As a child] we only had two bedrooms and I shared a four foot bed with three others. My son used to be always looking for his own bedroom here - I had four kids myself , and we had three bedrooms, and he didn't want to be sharing with his brother - but I said to him: 'Look, I never even had my own *bed*, not to mind my own room: I shared a bed, and I'm still sharing' And that's my party-piece, the joke at home about that.

I suppose I saw changes from the '50s to the 2000s, and a lot of places were left go derelict and everything, like. And it's lovely to see so much interest being paid in the city again, and for my own children and grandchildren to come, its lovely to see it's open to Europe so much, but you'd wonder will they ever have what we had - the old memories.

There is a big difference in the city centre - it's all come on and developed so much - but I love in my mind to wander along Cove Street, and look at the South Presentation Convent, and think of all the things that were, and the way buildings have changed. Government Buildings now in Sullivan's Quay, that was then Crosses Garage, and all the cars used to be out in the windows, and we used to love as kids going to see them, and where there is a big nightclub and bar there now it used to be the fire station. And I was thinking back when we were kids and we'd hear the fire station starting off, we'd chase after that fire engine, for as long as we'd go. There might be a fire in Ballyphehane or wherever, and we'd keep running after it to see where the fire was. And all these thoughts would be coming to my mind, as I'd be going along, and even along Sullivan's Quay,

Right: The angel, poised to give the people of Cork an exclusive warning.

Below: Sullivan's Quay today.

Noreen on her Confirmation Day.

where all the seats are, I could remember back, like, the old fishermen sitting there. And there was two or three men living in our area that were fishermen, and they would be kind of watching out for you if you were going too near the water's edge, or whatever, and he'd hunt you home, and he'd say he'd tell your mother on you.

They were a great people. Great sense of humour, everybody had stories to tell, great sense of humour. I have experienced both. I'm from the Southside: I'm longer living in the Northside than the Southside, so I suppose . . . am I an adopted Norrie? On both sides of the river as I'd say, they're great people; characters and grandparents, when you'd look back at them all, aunts and uncles and the stories and the yarns. I mean sometimes you could be a bit sad. I suppose I'm not old . . . I'm older but not old, like, but like when you look back on it, God sure that's all gone: all that was, is now gone. Where my father worked and my brothers and sisters worked, they'd be gone now; my own place where I worked, but sure I suppose that happens in all walks of life. So I have wonderful, wonderful memories. And we're expecting our first grandchild this year, and I hope they have many more, and then I will be able to sit down and tell them the stories and learn them the poems and the songs that were passed on to me down through the generations. It's all the good to come, like.

3

When We Were Young

We were all small once. Memories of that time have a particular resonance: it is a different view of the world from the one we have now. Much of it may be blurred, but some scenes, smells, tastes, emotions and people stand out: the excitement of a game well played, the intimate knowledge of favourite places, the special savour of a treat.

Our elders are there also: we bring the past generations with us. They say you're not truly dead until the last person who remembers you is gone. Any group of people has an unseen but present host with them, people who had an influence on their past and shaped them for the present and future, and the contributors to this book are no different. We are happy to have met some of these elders through the interviews.

Games

Liz Steiner-Scott

I was born in New Jersey, which is about an hour south of New York City. I grew up in a very middle class suburban neighbourhood, my parents moved there when they first got married in 1946, and I was born in 1948 … We played a game, it was kind of like a hide-and-seek game in the house, it was called 'sardines' in America. The person who was 'it' would have to count to ten with their eyes closed, and everybody would go out and hide. You moved from your own hiding place if you thought you were going to be found, and you went in with somebody else, and at the end of the game, like, ten of us would all be piled into one closet all together while the person was looking for us.

Stefan Wulff

I come from the Ruhr Valley in Germany and I was born in Dortmund, which is one of the biggest cities in the Ruhr Valley. There is another sister and another brother, both older than me. That house was a relatively new, detached house, and we had acres of space around. We all had our own garden, which wasn't that big, but we had plenty of fields. At that stage it would have been agricultural all around; the town was called Little Dortmund, and was one of the suburbs of Dortmund to the west.

We were up to quite a lot, there were a few other kids my age, so we would have roamed the fields, we would have made use of the street we were living in, which was

Above: The Wulff children and friend: Stefan is the second child from the left.

Right: Stefan launching a missile.

relatively quiet. It was all quite exciting, adventurous, and obviously we had our fights, we had our accidents, falling off our bicycles, being hit by missiles flying, the missiles we would have thrown at one another, it could have been soil or whatever else. We would have climbed trees, bow and arrow and all that, trying to shoot off the hats off the ladies walking by and getting into all sorts of trouble because of that. Yeah, it was a great time really.

Tim O'Brien

My mother came from West Cork: that was a favourite place that we'd always go, there was massive freedom down there, [that] there wasn't in the city. I remember one time my aunt decided I was old enough, and she told me go out and bring the cows from the field, and I thought I was very important. The cows knew where they were going, right. When I opened the gate, I just walked after the cows, but I thought I was very important, you know. There was a great sense of fun then with the people in the country as well, and I had the advantage of seeing the country people and the city people as I was growing up. I also had the advantage of the city, for the convenience of dances, youth club, cinemas. They would have been a big deal in the country, but they weren't a big deal in the city, so I could be a bit of a big shot when I went out the country, telling them about the films that I saw and stuff like that.

The favourite [game] that I remember was a game of hurling, but we didn't know much about hurling, as such. The hurley was more often than not turned into a rifle to play cowboys with. Then we'd have games where there'd be boys and girls and there'd be release, where you could have twenty or thirty people chasing in and out of a designated area, so when someone would shout, 'release,' everyone would run back out, and the team doing the chasing at the start would have to start all over again, and catch everyone. There was 'One, two, three, the book is red.' We lived in a terrace and it was kind of half a cul-de-sac so you'd have a person standing at the top end, and about fifteen or twenty people behind them, and once the person turned around and said, 'One, two, three, the book is red,' once their back was turned you could step forward, but you had to be stopped by the time [they turned back to face you], otherwise you had to turn back and start again.

I remember one game, all right, one of the older lads in the area played. He was one of the older fellas so we did what we were told, and he took a shine to a girl who lived in a house that was up a good bit away from us. He used to dispatch one or two of us little ones to go up and kind of watch, and when she'd come out of her house she had to walk down the road past where we lived, so as soon as she came out of the house and started heading down the road, we had to run down, knock on his door, he'd come out, and he'd be kicking the ball up against the wall when she'd walk by. And I don't think he ever actually spoke to her, but we definitely spent a couple of months running up and down to tell him when she was coming out, you know.

From Watercourse Road we used to go up out Blackpool, and then go up the Assumption Convent, and there was a walkway along there at the time, and then from there up into the Glen. You'd get a whole day out of the Glen, and it was a massive trip. If you were a bit more ambitious than the Glen, you went out as far as Garvey's Bridge, and up to Murphy's Rock. Murphy's Rock was a great place, we used to go out there picking

blackberries. You'd go out with a bucket or bags, you wouldn't come back until you were absolutely loaded. But sure, nobody makes jam now, so there's no point in picking the berries. Everything is kind of cheap and sterile and pressurised and nobody gets any fun out of it anymore. Murphy's Rock was a fabulous place, but now there's four housing estates in what was Murphy's Rock.

Eglinton Street swimming pool: we used to go to the baths. And that was a bit of an event because we were going into town, and there was concern if you were going into town. But then on the other side it was a lot safer, because any adult would give you a kick in the arse if you did anything out of the way, it didn't have to be your parent or know you. We used to come down from Blackpool to the baths, for young fellas it was probably about twenty-five minutes' walk. And however long it took us to come down, it would take us twice as long to go back because we would go to the Cork Cold Storage for the ice creams. I mean to say, the ice cream would take you half an hour to eat it, it was so big. And you would go home and you'd think that you were the flippin' prince of the world. And the whole thing for maybe three pence to get into the Eglinton Street baths, and another three pence going home, that's six pence.

Dearbhla Kelleher
I remember one Christmas all right, my relatives from England were over. My Mam and Dad were gone out and my older sister was babysitting us and we used to play chasing in the house, hiding behind curtains and under the chairs and everything, sure we used to hide in anywhere, and we had the whole house blackened. We used have a good laugh.

Right: Kay with her mother and brother and sister in Fitzgerald's Park in 1950. Kay is on the right.

Opposite: Dearbhla at home, Christmas day.

Patrícia Manresa

At school we used to collect eight stones, each of us, and then we would have our eight special stones and then there was ten different ways of throwing. The first step was you had to throw up a stone in the air, and while it was in the air you had to collect another stone. A few of my classmates and myself, we just sat around and played this game, and then the one that failed was out.

Kay O'Carroll

I was kind of a terror for playing out in the street, once I went out I never wanted to come in. Going picking blackberries in September, we'd go especially out Fairhill, like, you had all the hedging, and like that time you'd get beautiful blackberries. You know they'd be fine big bunters because you'd have gorgeous summers, we had sunshine from April to October. I used to love going out getting the blackberries, bringing them home in your little bucket, your seaside bucket or anything your mother would give you, then they would be washed and the apple put into them and they'd be boiled … and the smell, when you'd come in the door and get the smell, and you see you'd have fresh bread every day, that was my favourite, fresh bread and jam.

Up the park, I used to love Fitzgerald's Park, the slide, and then there was the Merries, the funfair, that would be up the Mardyke. I always dreaded the chairoplanes, I was always afraid of my life that it would break. But I used to love the swing-boats, you'd pull the rope and [go higher], I used to love that. I never had much dread, I was a little bit fearless growing up, but I can always remember that I was afraid of the chairoplanes.

Treats

Andy Hawkins
A treat for me as a boy growing up was a Saturday afternoon getting what I call a 'half a dollar' - two and six - from my mother. That was my pocket money. And I had to get it before lunchtime, you see, because like, the boys would have the picture picked out and there was usually two movies, and we'd always say 'who's the boy?' – who's the main character. And it was: 'he's the boy,' oh, Audie Murphy was the boy, so to speak, in the westerns. And if I missed out on that, gee … I'd get terrible down for the day.

Geoffrey D'Souza
Most of the time Indian celebrations and festivals would be related to your religion: I'm a Hindu by religion. It's a very colourful country: you go to a temple and you feed a cow, the cow is supposed to be a really holy animal, and killing a cow or eating a cow is supposed to be sacrilege. That would be my major remembrance about a family gathering; you would go to a temple, pray to God, and you would remember all the colours, festivities, people going crazy, monkeys crawling around the place. Obviously you won't see it anywhere else except India because India is the only country where you will see such a craziness going on anyway. It's like going to a church for your Communion and Confirmation, and you would remember that because of the huge crowd, and so many people and so many things happening … that would be my best memory.

Noreen Hanover
My older sister Helen, when she was seventeen or eighteen she was going with her now husband, Derry, and they'd go to the pictures on a Sunday night. And every single Monday night we used to go to bed early, that was always an early night for going to bed, the four of us, and she used to take us in and tell us the films, the whole story of the film, like. I remember one story, *Madame X*, it was about a woman, Lana Turner … oh we were roaring crying over it, like. So she would take us off into bed on a Monday night, and I would go to school and tell the girls in school [the next day]. I would be telling all the girls in my class that my sister went to see such a film, and you would be telling them during your lunch break at school, so we got great mileage out of the tickets.

Rob Stafford
I had a horse as a child, and I spent hours and hours riding the horse through the bush There was one place down by the river where we used to hang out down there and go fishing or whatever, bring the horse down there and tie him up for the day. One thing I really enjoyed was going camping out in the bush. I remember spending two weeks up in the Aboriginal community, up in the north west of Australia, and that really was a treat. They had a sheep station, basically, and I learned a lot from them. They have a brilliant sense of humour, much more fun than the white Aussies for sure. They are a very, very laid back bunch of people, very close community. Great fishermen: they're good at everything, basically. They still know how to do all those things [hunting and fishing], even though

Above left: Rob and his horse Springtop.

Above right: Kay in the First Communion dress her aunt decorated.

a lot of them live in towns. I mean they eat our food, but they also go out and hunt, supplement it, you know that's their thing … I was standing on a jetty and there were three white guys with fancy rods, fishing for king fish - they're about two foot long - with lures and the whole bit. You know, one of these rods, it would be worth about three hundred dollars, and this mate of mine, Ernie, another friend of his just had a hand line with a bolt tied on the end, and don't ask me how they did it, but they landed two king fish and the other guys didn't get anything…

Kay O'Carroll
Oh yes, we all remember the First Communion, going to the Church. My aunt was a dressmaker, and I remember my frock was bought at the top of Shandon Street, in Smart Wear. I remember my aunt putting two lacy pockets on my frock, it must have been a plain dress, and she put two lacy pockets, and she made me a coat that colour. She was a lovely dressmaker, she used to work in Dowden's. And after the church we all went back to the school for lemonade and cakes, sure that was a great treat, and you'd go down town then and the photographer would be down in Patrick Street, especially outside the Victoria Hotel. We all stood to get our photograph taken.

Mícheál Ó Geallabháin
One of the happiest memories I have, which wasn't a treat at all, was coming from school, and I was absolutely soaked to the skin, absolutely soaked. Everything was wet down to the vest, everything wet, [but] you were in a secure background, the fire was on, and the clothes being warmed by the fire, you put the warm clothes on you. That sense of belonging, that sense of being loved, being safe, of course you took it for granted.

Elders

Brigid Carmody
I was born in Cork. My father died before I was born, so there was my mother, my sister and me. We lived in Cork and then we travelled to Dublin for a while. We lived in a halting site in Dublin and when I was seven my uncles came to tell us my grandfather was sick. So we moved back to Cork again and I moved into the house with my grandfather and another cousin, and my mother carried on living in a caravan. I stayed there, I went to school from there, Turner's Cross School.

We had a great relationship, me, my cousin and my grandfather. He was tough, he wouldn't let anyone away with much. But when everyone was gone he was very father-like, to me and my cousin. He was very strict around his family, you couldn't do certain things, the girls had to be very careful … he was tough, but a lovable man at the same time.

He used to make copper buckets, and he used to have us holding the solder in the fire, burn the tops of our fingers with it, and he'd mend umbrellas for the neighbours, and we had copper buckets all over the house and jugs and everything and he'd be out the back with his anvil … he'd light a fire out the back and we'd go in and we'd burn the solder for him to heat it up. He used to give us five pence going to school every day, for to buy sweets or whatever on the way to school. Looking back now, five pence would get you nothing, but we were thrilled, delighted with ourselves and we going on.

We had to grow up very early because at that age, seven, eight years old, we'd get ourselves up in the morning, we'd dress ourselves, we'd have our breakfast and we'd go to school because obviously he wasn't able to do it. And we'd just come back then and one of the aunts would be there to cook a dinner for us. And I was quite happy there, my mother and sister lived in a caravan and I was quite happy to stay there with my grandfather and my cousin.

Stories told
[He'd be] mainly talking about the wagons and what a good life it was, and travelling around and just being able to pick up, get up one morning and say, 'Right, I am going somewhere else today.' Just pick up and go, not to have to worry about whether I am going to be towed away from here, there were no restrictions on it you know, and meeting other families … you'd mention someone, and he'd say, 'I knew his father and I knew his brother, and they did this and they did that,' and all stories like that. I remember my grandmother, she died before I went into the house, but I can remember her telling

stories about the pinny they used to wear and the buttons. They would swap buttons, and she could tell a story about every button she had on her pinny, who it came from, what family gave it to her, where they [were] now, whether they were dead or alive. That's the way [with] traveller women, they sit around the fire all night telling stories and the kids would be asleep under the wagon or in the wagon, and that was their life.

Mahbub Akhter

My grandmother from my father's side, she died maybe ten years ago. I used to visit her, she used to live in the village, so I used to go and visit her once in a year with my family, or by myself. It wasn't so far from my home, maybe around thirty miles, but the transportation wasn't great. We used to go by train from our home town to the village, and from there my grandmother, she would send someone to receive us. My grandmother told me quite a few stories about their life, how they grew up, what was the social structure during that time, because actually, although I'm from Bangladesh, my grandparents, both of them were born in India. During 1947 when the British left the subcontinent, then they split the whole region, India and Pakistan … so India will be mainly for the Hindus, and Pakistan will be mainly for the Muslims, but that's not the way it worked, so they say that all the Muslims, they have to go to either East Pakistan or West Pakistan, and all the Hindus have to go to India. So my grandparents, being Muslim, they had to migrate from India to Bangladesh … It was definitely a difficult time. They have quite a few relatives there. In fact I have more relatives in India than in Bangladesh. I haven't met them but my parents have.

Noreen Geaney

Halloween night, we'd have the brack all right, seed brack, with caraway seeds. Then the apple would be hanging from the ceiling, then the basin of water with sixpence inside in the water, and you would dive, put your head into the water and try and bring out the sixpence. And then 'blindman's buff': there would be a blindfold put on one of the family and the others would run around the house, or hide somewhere in the house, and the person with the blindfold would try to catch them. It would be a long night, Hallowe'en night, it would maybe two or three hours, but I used always remember my mother, God rest her soul, she used always lay the table on Hallowe'en night going to bed, because she said the dead would be around to eat. I'll tell you something now, I used to be terrified: I used not sleep that night waiting for the noise of the delft from the kitchen.

Robert Fourie

You know, as a child I have a memory of my grandfather … they had a vineyard, well not a huge vineyard, just, like, some grape trees out the front yard. The grapes were kind of draped over a frame where my grandfather used to park his car. He used to pick these grapes, and he had some kind of machine inside his garage that he was brewing wine illegally I think, and I remember them sitting outside in the courtyard, my father and my grandfather, having some of his own homemade wine and having a good old laugh … The other thing about my grandfather was he had a heart condition, and he was convinced that garlic would look after his heart, and chillies, and he used to grow

Noreen Geaney in 2005.

chillies and garlic out the back yard. He'd always be chomping on a clove of garlic, and he had the most terrible breath, so I knew when my grandfather was coming down the passage; you could just smell the garlic coming down. In South Africa, when you greet your grandparents and your parents, you kiss them, and I remember always, like, my grandfather saying 'hello' and giving us all a kiss, and as kids my brothers and sisters just thinking, 'Oh, no, he stinks of garlic,' and hating it whenever he wanted to give us a kiss. My grandfather played the organ as well, he had a Lowry organ that he used to play, and he played it really well. My father was very musical as well, and played the organ too, but my grandfather used to play the organ when we'd go over to visit … Yeah, I remember sitting as a child listening to him playing the organ, and them all having a good old spot of wine from my grandfather's illegal wine that he was making. I remember that as a very young child, I couldn't have been older than four or five.

Noreen Hanover
My father's mother always used to come to us on a Friday. She used go for her pension, and she used to have a shawl. [She was] a very, very small little woman, only 4ft 11, and the black shawl on her. And she'd be there when we'd come from school at half past twelve for our dinner, and she'd always buy us 'Peggy's Legs,' you know the rock, and we thought they were a great treat.

Robert aged four with his
first love, Ducky Doo.

Liz Steiner-Scott

I was very close to my grandparents on my mother's side, they lived within five miles of my parents always. I'd come home from school and I'd walk up the drive, and my grandmother would be there waiting for us to come home from school, and then just settling in waiting for my mother to come home from work. It's only now as a working person I think, God, it must have been awful for my mother to have to come home and find her mother there. My grandmother would be there, kind of putting her feet up and saying, you know, 'Lets have a drink, it must be time to have a drink now,' and it would be four thirty in the afternoon or something. My poor mother would be just coming home from work, tired after the day, but I never thought of it that way as a kid of course, I thought that was, you know, just normal. My grandmother would spend an hour or two at our house before she'd go home to her own house to get ready for when my grandfather came home from work. You see, my mother was young when she had me, she married at nineteen, she had me at twenty one, so we were quite close in age … my grandmother wasn't that old to me either.

My grandmother was a flapper in the twenties, she was a real party girl. You know, one of the new women who cropped her hair and wore short dresses and drank like a fish, and went to fraternity parties at universities and things like that. [At home] they were all into Cole Porter, and George Gershwin, and show music. My parents went to theatre a lot in New York, they'd buy records and play show music.

Lily Xiong, right, and Ge Hei
in Cork, 2005.

We heard loads of stories, although of course now, as a historian, I wish I had asked
more growing up. You know, we'd always hear the stories of their parents, who were all
immigrants to the States, how they all came to the States, where they came from, how
they came with nothing, you know. My grandmother's parents all died before I was born,
so I didn't know them, but I'd hear all their stories. My [other] great-grandmother lived
until I was about ten, so she was in her nineties when she died. Grandma Olga, she came
from Latvia, from Riga, and she would tell us stories. They were anxious to come to
America, make their life in America, so they didn't really want to talk about what it was
like before they left, but you would hear those stories alright.

Lily Xiong

In my house at Spring Festival, we first we put all the lights on. My parents live with my
grandfather and grandmother, and my father has a brother, so on that day my uncle comes
to us. My uncle brings his family, my mother and my aunty cook the dumplings and then
my grandmother, my grandfather, my father, me, and my uncle, we sit down and watch
television. We have good fun. We get some candy, tea, we get some special Chinese snacks
before dinner. After that we watch a Chinese programme, a special show for Spring Festival
day [a big show that everyone watches]. There's dancing, music, singing, the traditional
Chinese songs, funny stories that make people laugh, and famous people coming.

Rob practising the fiddle, 1981.

Ge Hei
It lasts for hours, from seven to twelve, and at twelve o clock everyone is waiting for [the count down]. Ten, nine, eight, seven … then 'Happy New Year.' Then I will go to my grandmother, grandfather [and bow] and say, 'Happy New Year,' and then my grandmother and grandfather will give me money in a red bag.

Rob Stafford
I grew up near Perth, in Western Australia, a place called Karragullen, it would be about an hour and a half from Perth. It's an orchard district basically, well it was mostly forest, eucalyptus forest, state forest we call it, and then in the valleys there were orchards and that was the main income there – apples, and pears and stone fruit. There would be a lot of timber houses, brick and tile, verandas you know, corrugated iron roof, that kind of thing. There would be fires every year. It could get up to 45° C, one day it was 48° in the shade – that was a record day, but it can be 40° for two or three weeks.

I have no Irish relatives, but I grew up with the Irish community in Australia from an early age, they were almost a family to me, and one family in particular I spent most weekends in their house. The father was a fiddle player from Charlestown in Co. Mayo, and he taught me to play the fiddle, and we became friends. He was teaching a lot of children the fiddle, and he had a céili band, so I was part of the céili band.

I started playing around eight. My next door neighbour, a man called Eddie Lowe - he was an Australian Irishman, if you know what I mean - was a fiddle player, and his wife played the concertina. I used to go there each week and learn off him and then from there I progressed and met Sean Doherty – the man from Charlestown.

He was a lovely man, he still is. He grew up on a farm in Charlestown and his father played the fiddle. He was a very, very patient man. Every Friday night I'd go there, and I'd be there for three or four hours and he would be teaching me three or four tunes and he would just keep going and going and going until I got them. Then we'd listen to records quite often after that, and I'd stay there and be there for the whole weekend, and we'd go over the tunes again. He was big into the different styles around Ireland, and explaining … this would be the Kerry style, this would be the Donegal style, this would be the Sligo style, and of course, until I came to Ireland, it didn't really make sense. He would often play me records of Paddy Canny, PJ Hayes, these guys.

I learned that the music was more about people - was as much about people as music. That the whole thing of the session is more than just a bunch of tunes, which I think a lot of the Aussies seem to think it is. So it's more about who you learned the tune off, or whatever, and the people involved, the different styles, just the whole thing of enjoyment and tradition.

Well, I came to Ireland first when I was seventeen, basically because Sean Doherty put the idea in my head that I should go over for a summer and go to the Willy Clancy Week, and go round a few of the festivals. So I did that, and I ended up staying a year and a half,

Right: Adam in Cork, 2005.

Opposite: Rob and Sean Doherty in Perth, 1993.

and then I went back to Australia for two years, but I've been back ever since, so I've lived in Kerry, Macroom, Co Cork, and I've been in Galway for three years. For years now I've wanted to study violin making, and a year ago I moved to Cork to study with a French man called Betrand Galen, to study violin making, and that's what I'm doing.

Adam Skotarczak
[My grandfather] was a good man. I remember my grandfather, he teach me a lot about what man can do at home to repair something, fix something if something is broken. He teach me a lot what you can do in the garden - how to plant trees, flowers, grass, vegetables. He showed me how to sow vegetables into ground. He told me a lot of stories about his childhood, what he did during the war. He was a child, he worked on some German farm, so he didn't fight, he was a worker. He could fix everything. He taught me a lot about this - how to fix your bike, how to fix a chair. If something's broken in the house, he fixed it. He died a few years ago, but for all my life I remember him, he lived with us.

4

Emeka Ikebuasi

Emeka Ikebuasi

I was born in the northern part of Nigeria; Kaduna state. [In our neighbourhood] the houses are really clustered around with no places for children to play; we actually play in between the houses when you visit one another. We played football on the streets. We also have the other games. We call [one game] *moji-moji*, whereby a child is blindfolded and you have to run around to see how effectively you can spot another child who is hiding away from you. And once you get that, that person takes the turn to do the *moji-moji* while you also go into hiding. Amongst the girls, they have what you call *ogá*, whereby you clap hands and you make heart shape drawings on the ground. Usually the girls stay in opposite directions, clapping their hands and trying to switch their legs in between. One person will actually see how fast you can be able to determine the next step the other girl is trying to take. And, when you are able to catch her in that, you have beaten her and you start all over again. That's the way it runs.

Toys are not commonplace. But we tried to devise things, you know, from a little understanding or from the elders, who could make up things to play with. We normally rolled bicycle tyres, get a stick and hit them, take a run with bicycle tyres. Because of the setting, we did what we could easily reach out to that wouldn't involve spending money to do, because the money wasn't really there.

Weddings

There are two weddings that we do in Nigeria. First of all, you have the traditional wedding. In the traditional wedding, you know, you take your time to prepare. The families of the man and the families of the woman have to be in contact before this time and then they choose a date and, once that date has been confirmed, invitations are issued and preparations begin in earnest. There will be cultural dances, there will be a lot of food, from the native delicacies to normal meals of rice and stew or the fried rice and, the curry rice or the salads … whatever that person chooses. But there must be the normal native delicacies - and those ones are non-negotiable - because, if you don't have them, the elders will see the wedding as not fit to be rated as a wedding, so to speak. So you must have all that in place. And you will go out to invite your cousins, your brothers, your sisters, in-laws and whatever; they all will be there to give you a hand. But I think, like, here you have to contract out, like in the weddings that I have seen here.

Emeka with his wife Blessings at their wedding in Nigeria, just after drinking the palm wine.

Usually, the food has to be prepared by the families. And they will have input from neighbours who will come: they will bring food and the normal palm wines. Like, in the village where the woman is coming from, the members of that village, maybe everyone has to bring a keg of palm wine, a drink that comes from the palm tree. The drink is being tapped from the palm tree, and it comes out sweet and usually, when it's left to ferment, it comes out strong. But when you have the fresh one that has been tapped for the day it's, you know … it builds up gradually, the intoxication, you know, it's gradual.

Dress would be traditional for the traditional wedding. And then, there will be the time when the parent or the elder in the family where the woman is coming from would actually pour the palm wine into her mug. Then the elder or the father of the woman will now drink from the cup, give to his daughter and then ask her now, before the whole people gathered, to go round and locate her husband-to-be and present that palm wine to him, so that he can drink from it. And both of them will now walk up to the elder or the father of the woman and then present themselves. And he will give them the blessings before the whole people gathered and say: 'Now it is confirmed that this is the man who my daughter is getting married to.' And everybody – well, the whole villagers and neighbours and brothers and kinsmen – all will be party and witnesses to that. That, actually, is the main wedding to us. The white wedding – or the church wedding – is a place for, you know, just to show off, when you have that much to spend. But when the marriage or the wedding has consent of both families, it is usually portrayed at the traditional wedding.

Emeka and family in 2004 in the Baptist Church on MacCurtain Street. From left to right: Daniel, Ezra, Blessings with the baby Ebube, Eunice and Emeka.

Family

I grew up in a home where I had four girls before me and then I had five other kids behind. The first four all got married before the problem that we had in the year 2000, the religious riots that burnt the family house and meant … well everybody, we all lived differently because we were all …

My father worked for thirty-six years with the telecoms and when he retired he was able to build up my family home for us, through his pensions, and the family house was big and everybody was accommodated. And before I got married, I also lived in the family house. Later I started up my own business, after my education, and I was able to take care of the family house through the business where I was. So, that's the way it ran until we all had to go different places in 2000. As it is today, my parents, they had to relocate to an obscure village now, and my younger brothers are all in the southern part of Cameroon.

The house was burnt down in 2000. The militants, because there was … the people or the government of Kaduna state allowed Sharia law to be introduced and that spelt that that was to be the legal way for which cases will be determined. And the Christians kicked against it. The Christian Union led a peaceful demonstration to the government house in Kaduna state. While on their way back they were attacked. That actually triggered off a kind of a religious … it now had a religious configuration because the Christians had to defend themselves. And one of the Muslims and all the fundamentalists - they were called - resorted to bombing down of churches and houses of Christians in the state and that affected us. Everybody ran because we had to save our lives. We ran to different places to seek refuge. A lot of people were killed, a lot of people. We had corpses lying all over the streets of Kaduna State and it took the local council about two weeks to clear all that into mass graves. It was … it was a horrible sight, you know, but people were exposed to it at that time. So that was the way it went. It was a sad story but, all the same, I'm happy to be alive today.

Arrival in Ireland

When we got into Dublin on the seventh of November 2002, we were taken up to the refugee office. When we got there, we were taken in and asked a few questions. We were all fingerprinted and photographed. And that evening, there was a bus came and took a whole lot of us to a centre, in Finglas. We stayed there for a week and two days before we got a letter saying to us that we have to be moved over to Cork and … that was how I came to Cork with my family. When we got into Cork, we were moved into a centre in Glounthaune. When we got in … I remember the Christmas of 2002, there was this family: his name is Walter and his wife's name is Mary; they kept visiting us and they came with a lot of gifts, you know, toys for my children. It was a great, a big kind of reaching out to us and we were happy about that.

Well, I live up in Carrigaline and I found Carrigaline to be a home. But then, if I try to feel what Ireland is or what Cork is, I think there are a couple of places I have always gone to, and also taken my kids to. I have been up in Crosshaven, you know, watch all the people, like, when you have the festivals, you know, and also have the opportunity to be up in Robert's Cove, and it's a beautiful sight and there's a good beach. Apart from these other places, I also will be happy always to be in MacCurtain Street. That's the way I go up to church, the Baptist Church.

Drawing a comparison between Cork and a city in Nigeria, the cities in Nigeria are much bigger, you know, with a larger population and so much activities of people up and down and well, there is much more security here in Cork than any city or any state in Nigeria. Safer as in violence … I think you get little reports, here and there, which is of no consequence, you know, compared to what happens in some states in my country. And that to me is a plus for Cork, because that's the most important thing: when people can sleep and wake up and find their heads where they left it. There are some places where you sleep and you don't find your head. But here in Cork, for these past years, I know that, when I sleep, and when other people sleep they wake up and find their heads where they left them…

What I don't like about …

I cannot really say that, 'there is this I don't like about Cork,' because that will… it will put me in a corner as someone who is an ingrate. But, inasmuch as in every setting there must be the good, the bad and the ugly, to me, I don't see the people of Cork being discriminatory. I seldom hear people talk about it neither have I witnessed that. The only thing that might need a little fine tuning is the … well, I think I may need some time, but all the same … well, it happens everywhere, like, as in class differentials, class distinctions, people trying to place themselves above others saying, 'We are this, you are that,' but outside from all that, you know, the usual problems that will normally happen and will be evident in every society and in every setting. I think, aside from all that, Cork is grand to me, like the Irish people all say.

Emeka outside Cork Baptist
Church on MacCurtain
Street.

The rain

Just like today, now. It was pretty hard getting out of the house, coming out this way to
you for this interview ... it's been raining all day. But then, the rain is an act of God, it's
not manmade, so the Corkonians can't do anything about it. And neither will the mayor
of Cork do anything about it. So it's something that is way out of our hands. In my
country there are times when you have funny weather conditions and you still have to go
out and do whatever you want to do; it's a lazy man who will give reasons for maybe the
things that are God made. Because the rain is doing its job and you ought to go out and
do your own job. So, that's the way I see it, to me it's not a problem.

Change in Cork

Cork is developing at a faster rate and things are happening, you know, dramatically. There
are a lot of changes that I witnessed and the people are committed to, you know, their
ideals. Maybe that's the reason they're called 'the rebels,' because they stick to whatever
they believe in, they don't seem to waver ... I think they don't compromise. And I find
that challenging, when people will mean something and keep to it, live by it. I see the
spirit in them whenever there is a match between Cork and any other city like the last

one with Kilkenny [the All-Ireland hurling final, 2004]. When I came out to the city centre, the whole place, the whole roads and streets were closed. And I was asking; and I was told [it was] because Cork won. And I said, 'That's great!' People wanting to identify with their people. It's a whole lot of encouragement to all the people, all the lads who went up and represented Cork. And, if I were one of them, I think I'll be moved to put in more effort and see that I have people behind me who are actually proud of what I was doing: definitely, I want to invest more into the city. It's one thing that I like about Cork.

African food
When we want to buy the African food, there are a lot of African shops: on Shandon Street, and there's one on Grattan Street, and another one by the traffic lights between MacCurtain Street and the next street. So there are a couple of them; and another one on Barrack Street. And on Shandon you have Crystals [Super Stores]; and then on Pope's Quay you have Chuky Dandy and off North Main Street there is another African shop. A lot of the local delicacies … all the ingredients and the spices. We all get them there, at those shops. They go to a lot of lengths to get all that stuff across.

The chicken never forgets that person who prunes his wings during the rainy season.
[Talking about an intercultural group he was part of at the time] But the idea behind the group is not just to organise events for people to socialise, but it's … we see that there *is* a need to change the perception and the bias that some people may have - or that some people have. I have heard some words, you know, in some quarters; people when they refer to the minorities as 'spongers.' Some people will say, 'These people are no-goods and they are here just to mess up the place and after that they will leave.' Just to change all that, and let them know that, when you go to a place to seek refuge, when you run to a place, like - there is a proverbial saying, in my part of the country; 'If a child is being pursued, he runs into a place of safety and that place of safety becomes his home.' And another one says, 'The chicken never forgets that person who prunes his wings during the during the rainy season.' During the rainy season it's usually messy for the chickens when their wings get dirty and wet, so, when they are pruned down, that person is looking after them. So it goes to say that you don't forget that person who takes you in and looks after you when you are in time of need. That is what we intend to change by, you know, the idea of the Cork Intercultural Group. We want to see this as a way of reaching out to the people because all of us cannot come at the same time in one voice to say: 'Thank you, Ireland, for sheltering us, for taking us in and for showing us all love and care.' With this, the way we are doing volunteering works, that is the reason why we are doing all this, until every man and every woman and every child in Ireland understands that the minorities who are here are part of us and they mean good. We don't say that there are no exceptions - there are some exceptions - people who can be dubious, people who can go on the wrong side and do things that are against the law, but it's not only the Africans who can do that; it's usually everywhere. All we are saying is that a larger number of us are committed to the Irish dream and we want to see that happen, and we want to call Ireland home.

Getting used to Cork forms of communication

When I got into the bus - and while we were alighting from the bus - the locals were going down and I would hear each one say to the driver, 'Thanks a million.' And I wondered: 'Why would you say "thank you" to the driver?' I supposed maybe they didn't pay their fare. And it was one day I was talking to one of the managers at the centre, so I asked … and he said, 'Usually, when a thing is done for you in Ireland, even when you don't find it as a favour, that saying "thank you" goes a long way and it makes a whole lot of meaning. It finds a path into one's heart on your behalf when you say "thank you" or "thanks a million" and all that.' So I said, 'Well, yeah, it's good to appreciate when the driver has driven the bus well, and then you got to your destination safely. It's proper to say thank you.' And that was another lesson for me.

Yeah. Even when they're not happy about something, they can say, 'It's grand, you're grand, you're grand. That's perfect.' At times they might criticise that, but before they would always say, 'It's grand, it's grand. Oh, perfect, grand job!' And all that … So, when I got to understand that, I said, 'Well, I mustn't get carried away when I hear, 'Perfect, grand job!' I will also have to take time and look round myself and see that I am getting it right. Not to be carried away by those words.

It's commonplace when you hear Cork people say, 'Oh, thanks, love,' and, 'You know, like' and a lot more phrases that I just can't remember now … It's becoming part of us now that we also have to use and be part of Cork, you know? But the accent is something that might take us time to get into; well, except with our kids, because they grew up with children who definitely influence their own accent. But for us adults it's not going to be easy, but then, we're getting there … gradually.

Nawen

It would amaze you the amount of people I have known, that I have shared good times with: people who have a heart of understanding, of care, and a heart of love. It amazes me, the openness with which they have welcomed me and all that I represent, and they have also tried to share my pain and my moments of joy, and they have always tried to encourage me to live up to my dreams, and never waver, never give up, always see myself as achieving and getting there.

People in Cork reach out easily to minorities more than other places; I know that from what I hear. I don't see Ireland as a racist state, so to speak, but there are exceptions, you know, people who might go out of their way to do things, which aren't the stance of the state. I think Cork is a place where people actually carry out the message that we all have to reach out to minorities, make them a part of us, encourage them in any way that we can, and make them feel happy and feel good. And the people in my church, especially my pastor, pastor Terry and his wife Pat, and other members of his church.

Three words that would describe Cork? Well, if I was to give it back to you the same way that the people in Cork would say: Cork is perfect, and Cork is grand, and Cork is beautiful, like. In my language I can always say to the people, *nawen,* that is to say: 'Thank you so much.'

5

Paths to Cork

How do people end up coming to Cork? Here are just a few accounts of the various paths to the city.

B. O'D.

I never thought I would end up in Ireland. What happened … I met this man in London, and I couldn't stay away: I went back home for a year, and couldn't stay away so I came and said I'd give it a try in Cork. That was the whole reason why I came here. I knew very little about it apart that it's raining three hundred days in the year, which I wasn't glad about.

Arriving: I remember it was a weird story, because I came here three days and three nights on the bus, going from my town to Prague and from Prague to London, and I planned to stay in London for a day just to see my friends but everything went completely wrong and the buses broke down on the way, so I didn't get to meet anybody. I got to Rosslare eventually, and I was looking: 'this is Ireland, 'tis all green.' I think the first thing I spotted was that the houses were so colourful, in my country in Slovakia they're not as colourful. The fog of course was there, and I came to Cork on the bus, to the bus station, and I met with my husband. I had spent about two years in London and I thought I had good English, and I went down to a pub and the first night, I remember with a group of people from Cork, and I was just sitting in the middle looking at them; it was OK when I was talking with somebody one-to-one but when there was a group talking I didn't know; it took me three weeks before I could actually understand the accent.

Stefan Wulff

Well I would have come to Cork the first time in 1983, that was in the context of a cycling holiday. I think at the time Ireland was very much on my generation's agenda. There were all sorts of romantic ideas about it, and I suppose the music would have been very influential: the Dubliners and Clannad, Davey Arthur and so on, and so many people would have come back and said, 'This is just a marvellous country, and great for holidays, and great for cycling.' So a group of friends decided we want to go on a cycling holiday, and we were under the illusion that we probably were among the few who did it by bicycle. So we arrived at the airport, and there were hundreds of them: everybody was quite comical, in that the lobby of Frankfurt airport was littered with bicycles. So we

Stefan, in the stripey shirt,
with his brother and sister a
few years before his first trip
to Cork.

arrived into Dublin, did our tour all along the coast, and cycling along the south coast
brought us into Cork. I think we only stayed one night here, and we stayed in a youth
hostel down in Western Road. What left an impression on me at the time was, a friend of
ours who had been in Ireland a year before, she got to meet the daughter of a family who
lived here in Cork, somewhere up in Sunday's Well. This friend of ours, she contacted her
friend, who in turn invited us to her house. Actually she wasn't there, only her parents.
They were a bit surprised because they didn't know about that bit, nevertheless they
invited us in. And just to come into that house: the house was quite big and extremely
disorganised, so it was just the parents. They were both quite elderly, and very friendly,
and so they tried to make the best of the situation as they could. They had this dog, a
Kerry sheepdog, who was quite a bit of a lunatic: he always wanted to play, and there was
a ball, and he would throw the ball through the house, and he would catch it, and in the
background the television was on, with *Knight Rider* and all that. We were impressed with
the idiosyncrasies of the parents as we perceived it, [as] people who were quite unfamiliar
with the Irish way of living and sayings and phrases and so on. So eventually after a
while, the daughter arrived, and we had some meal in the house. And I still remember
the sausages – I had never seen them before, they were the small cocktail sausages – and

I suppose because we were cycling all the time we were always very hungry, and they looked like they weren't going to be sufficient sustenance for the next while. We got over that: it was a great experience.

From the beginning I liked Cork because of the Lee: I always have this liking for cities where there is a river running through it. It was another eleven years before I came back, and that was in the context of a student exchange programme. I was studying in Dortmund, and they gave us the opportunity to go abroad wherever you wanted, and I picked Ireland. I could have chosen between Dublin and Cork, and so because I come from quite a big city, I wanted to get away from that, and I opted for Cork, and that is how I ended up here.

The exchange originally was meant to last half a year only, so I got a placement here, but I also went to UCC [University College, Cork], and did some studies, and I was just blown away. I had a great time, I met very nice people on the course, very sociable so there was great craic, more or less twenty four hours a day, and then I met my wife-to-be in a parallel course, and I suppose one thing led to another. I applied for a transfer from my university over to UCC to finish my studies here, and so it worked out, and I am pretty much settled here.

I suppose the initial time coming here on a placement, being in UCC, studying a little bit, but by and large having a very good time, deluded me to quite an extent: that was not the real thing. Starting in UCC properly, now that had an implication on my language abilities: in the beginning I found it difficult enough to follow things, and then more difficult to get assignments done. I remember I was tired all the time, and I suppose after a while there was a stage when I was quite resentful of being here, because it meant a lot of energy had to be put into it, I felt drained all the time, an accumulation of things really. And then I suppose the realities of living in Ireland, as opposed to being a guest in Ireland, was quite a contrast. I'm a trained social worker, and so obviously I would have had a very good insight into social affairs in Irish society or in Cork society, which certainly helped a lot, but at the same time at times could make things appear far more bleak than they probably were. The kind of situations that I dealt with, or had to deal with, it could drag me down a fair bit, and just the social dimensions were very much different than what I would have been used to in Germany. I come from pretty much a middle class background, and it didn't have much to do with what I am doing now actually, and so that took a fair bit of settling down, but I suppose over the years, it literally took me years to find my place. It's working out quite well now.

Liz Steiner-Scott
I've been in Ireland for 30 years, and I've been in Cork for 27 years of those 30 years. We always say that, in the bad old days when everybody was leaving Ireland, we were the few that were coming into Ireland, and Ireland was always very good to us.

Jeff had the interview for the job in July of 1976, early July, it was a hot day. I came down from Dublin, I had never been to Cork. I remember I brought my camera: we never thought we would end up in Cork, so I wandered around the city while he was having his interview, like a tourist, taking pictures. In those days Cork was really grim - it hadn't been redone, there were lots of derelict buildings. I remember coming in from

Liz in her office in UCC, 2005.

the train station, we must have taken a bus into Patrick Street from the train station. In those days Merchant's Quay was all boarded up and run down, and I wandered into the English Market, which also hadn't been done up yet, and it was stinking on a hot day, and I just thought Cork was a kip. I thought Cork was small, and not very nice, not very clean, and we got on the train going back to Dublin that day, and we did our pros and cons, you know how you do for a job, and the only pro was that it was a job: I couldn't see myself living here.

And then he got the job, and of course we came because it was a job, and I have to say my first year in Cork was tough. When you first come in, particularly in those days … it was really only after I had my daughter in 1978 that Cork became more comfortable for me. I also got involved in the Women's Movement, and I was very involved in organising the Rape Crisis Centre and things like that, and then everything started to click, but in the very, very early years Cork is a tough place to come into if you're not from there. I had my daughter in St. Finbarr's, and we were living out behind the airport on a dairy farm at that point, and people were lovely up there, and I really felt totally comfortable after that - I mean there was no question then of even thinking about going back to Dublin, and I never thought about going back to the States.

Stephen Wimpenny
I grew up in Yorkshire in England, I was born in Yorkshire, bred in Yorkshire, and lived there till I was eighteen years old and went to university. Before I came over to Cork I was actually working in Orkney, which is an island way, way off the north of Scotland. I was still seeing my friends from Yorkshire. Now, one of my friends, he works in the IT industry, and he got free flights over to Cork one weekend to do a job, so I came over

Stephen at work in
Northside Community
Enterprises.

with him. And when we were over – this was three, four years ago now – we decided to
do the Midleton Distillery tour. So we went up to Midleton, and did the tour, sampled
the whiskey, and we thought, 'this is quite a nice small town,' so we stayed around and
we went into a place called McDaid's for a drink. One drink led to another and we were
having a great time in there, and I was chatting to some of the local ladies, one of whom
is now my wife: she took my eye, I took her eye. So I went back over to Scotland, to
Orkney, and we were corresponding, and maybe two or three times a year we would
meet up in Edinburgh or London, wherever was halfway between us. One thing led to
another, it got kind of serious, and it got kind of expensive as well seeing each other, so
we were discussing would Áine come over to Orkney, and would I go to Cork. Orkney
is such a small place – there'd be more opportunities in Cork – so I ended up coming
over in January 2002, we became engaged, and we were married in August 2003. So that's
how I'm here.

First impressions of Cork
Very small in terms of city size – coming from the UK the cities seem to be much larger
– but also very friendly. I guess with it being smaller and more compact, there is more of
a friendly ambience, and people seem to give you more time than they would do back in
the UK. Back home you'd get a 'hello, goodbye' type of thing, but people are prepared to
stop and chat and you'd see people chatting on street corners, in shops etc. The word that

would encompass Cork as a city would be 'friendly,' a real friendly down-to-earth city.

What do I find difficult? I would say – maybe an adjustment rather than a difficulty – would be the driving: the driving over here is completely different to back home in the UK. People seem to know where they're going, and everybody else seems to know where they're going, and there's not necessarily many indicators going on. So the driving would be the main difficulty, but now I'm just the same.

I think the whole Irish culture is so different from a UK culture, [but] I think the people of Cork are very, very similar to the people of Yorkshire – they're really, really down-to-earth, salt-of-the-earth type people.

6

Yossi Valdman

My name is Yossi Valdman and I live in Cork. I grew up in a town [in Israel] just about a mile from Jaffa, called Bat Yam. My father's store is situated there. He used to have a big cooler of frozen beef, and I grew up working in the shop part time and living in Bat Yam. It's a kind of a sea resort as well, [a] tourist town, we get loads of tourists during the summer. The place where I grew up, it's kind of rough, you know, it's co-op houses and they are kind of high houses; we used to live in the fifth floor of an eight-storey building. The difference is that we have loads of balconies and everybody comes out to the balcony and everything is way kind of out in the open. The sea was very near, it's about five minutes' walk from the house, so I used to go a lot to the sea, where I used to be fond of swimming. There was a lot of crime and, do you know, socially it was just like every other city in the world I think.

My father, Aron, is a Second World War survivor, [he] managed to drift to Israel in 1947, a very strong man, and a very hard-working man. If he was drinking until two o'clock in the morning he'll get up at four o'clock and go to work, open the shop in the market. My mother, Freda, as well a Second World War survivor, no-one of her known family left, none that she can remember. She used to work in the family store as well, a very hard-working woman. They are both military trained, my parents, and very strong people.

We weren't very religious even though my father says that my grandfather was a semi-rabbi. We used to meet a lot at something that dad use to say *gratar* in Romanian, which is a grill, barbecue, a big picnic, you know and usually it used to be taken in swimming pools or balconies. Dad has six brothers and sisters and we used to meet, you know.

I used to like playing drums a lot and music since I was very young. I was really a dreamer. My teenage years used to really be obsessed with Rock'n Roll music, obsessed. You know, even when I heard Thin Lizzie I thought they were American at the time. [I listened to it all], having a whole collection of Rock'n Roll music, Beatles, Rolling Stones. That was until I went to the army at the age of eighteen … that was the time I start being serious really, and practical.

When I was released from the army I always wanted to move out of Israel, to be a musician. That was the first aim and objective of my life, really. I worked in a melon farm in unoccupied territory of Nueba, for the settlers. It was very good to save money and to live, like, free in a sea resort do you know, with no obligation. 'Till I met my wife, Margaret, she was from Ireland. And we decided to travel together, so we did, and I ended up here.

Above left: Yossi aged two.

Above right: Yossi at his sister Sara's Bat Mitzvah in the 1960s.

Left: Yossi's father Aron in 1976.

Left: Yossi aged 15.

Below: Yossi with his first girlfriend, aged 15.

Playing Jazz in 2005.

Well I came to Ireland in 1981, that was the very day one of the hunger strikers died, Mr. Patsy O'Hara. It was very sad, and I kind of started being introduced to Ireland from that aspect, and for me it was like a bang in the head, really. And I've learned a lot about Ireland since, and I've learned to adore the people, really, and, the passion, the way they live, the way they hide emotions … 'Ah, everything is going to be alright,' the craic, music, *ceol* and, I've leant a lot in this Irish music.

I came to Cork city three years ago and after applying to the Cork Academy of Music. And when I got the course I just moved to Cork. Cork was a big question mark for me as well. I find Cork very different [to] all Ireland, really. It's really cosmopolitan, a different kind of Irish people, different kind of way of speaking. Some people, I can't understand them, and I wonder if they speak English or not. But [I've] been living there for three years, do you know it was just a wonderful experience, really a most beautiful experience I had.

When I came to Ireland, you know, my English was quite bad. I could speak English like, quite flatly. It used to be a barrier of culture, but when I came here I was very, if you like, very open, very, do you know, very fast in many things. People didn't like it, or people were afraid of it. I used to call to people's houses and kind of, do you know, where in Israel people have to call to people's houses [it's not expected here]. There are a lot of things where [there are differences], like if we had a packet of cigarettes here on the table, you know, I'll take a cigarette, knowing that you are my friend, and there is no problem. In the bar, for instance, we order our drinks and we pay as we leave. In Ireland you pay

1 From left to right: Catherina McCarthy, Jessica O'Reilly and Nikita O'Brien on George's Quay.

2 Street acrobats on Patrick's Bridge during the 2005 St Patrick's Day parade.

3 *Left:* Dennehy's fish shop, Blackpool.

4 *Right:* A Coal Quay trader.

5 *Right:* Brigid Carmody with a pinny like the one her grandmother used to have.

6 *Below:* The Barrel Top Wagon in the St Patrick's Day parade 2005.

7 *Left:* Barrel Top Wagon on Bridge Street on St Patrick's Day 2005.

8 *Right:* From left to right: Kathleen Collins, Eileen St Leger and Norah Rahilly on Kyle Street.

9, 10 & 11 *Opposite page:* Cork newspaper vendors.

12 *Above:* Rob Stafford as a child.

13 *Left:* Yossi Valdman's parents.

14 *Above:* Noreen Hanover's family on her mother's eightieth birthday. Noreen is standing third from the right. Her sister Rose is standing first on the left, and her sister Helen, who used to 'tell the pictures' on a Monday night, is standing third from the left.

15 *Right:* Liz Steiner-Scott (left) and her interviewer Frances Quirke at the launch of *How's if goin', boy?* radio programmes in 2005.

16 *Left:* Emeka Ikebuasi and his wife
Blessings at their wedding in Nigeria.

17 *Below:* Emeka Ikebuasi and his wife
Blessings with her mother and sister at their
wedding.

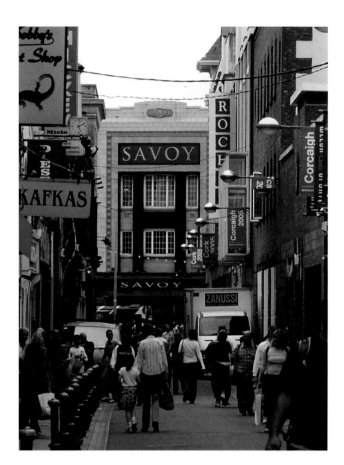

18 *Right:* The Savoy from Maylor Street.

19 *Below:* At the Port of Cork.

20 *Left:* Grafitti artist, Dex.

21 *Right:* The Shakey Bridge.

22 *Above:* Pope's Quay.

23 *Right:* Three Roma women outside St Peter and Paul's.

24 *Above:* Contributors and interviewers at the launch of the *How's it goin', boy?* radio programmes in the Vision Centre, North Main Street, June 2005. From left to right, Back row: Marie-Annick Desplanques, Billy McCarthy, Rob Stafford, Stefan Wulff, Marcus Bale, Vitaliy Mahknanov, Robert Fourie, David Walker, John Mehegan, Andy Hawkins, Dolores Horgan, Cliona O'Carroll. Front row: Jenny Butler, Isabelle Sheridan, Dearbhla Kelleher, Frances Quirke, Noreen Hanover, Mahbub Akhter, Yossi Valdman, Ge Hei, Lily Xiong, Alan Botan.

25 *Left:* Alan Botan and a friend at the launch.

26 *Above:* From left to right: Alan Botan, Noel O'Shaughnessy, Mahbub Akhter, Andy Hawkins, Rob Stafford.

27 *Right:* Stefan Wulff and his interviewer Mary O'Driscoll.

28 Cork City Hall.

29 Patrick's Street by night.

30 *Right:* A Patrick Street scene.

31 *Below:* The Grand Parade during restructuring.

32 A Kyle Street shop window.

33 Kathleen Collins, Eileen St Leger and Norah Rahilly on Kyle Street.

Yossi with his sister Sara in 1962.

now, you know. And things like that. Do you know, it used to make me angry, but like, the Irish people kind of advised me, 'That's the way we live,' and you know 'there is nothing we can do about that now.'

Ireland in comparison with Israel
First of all it's very cold, and it *is* different. It is very religious in many ways. It is very political, which is kind of a major factor. I find young people a bit, em … undisciplined, you know, drinking too much and the trouble is that they cause, you know, other results of drink. The difference here [is] that somebody can go to a judge and just say, 'I was too drunk and therefore I behaved the way I behaved,' where in other places I don't think it would be an excuse: if you don't know how to drink, just don't drink. You know, if you can't handle a drink, obviously you have a problem; you have to tackle that problem, why you cannot enjoy a drink.

Israel is very cosmopolitan, and you've got people from I think 72 nations, Jewish people, then you've got Christian people as well from every nation. It's very small and still it doesn't feel very cramped, you know, as small as we are, and then you got our brothers, the Palestinians, and you find every race, every colour there, you know. I can see Ireland being like that as well, which is going to be so beautiful. You know, when you're going to get a second generation of Romanian or Slovakian or anything, swing the ball for Ireland [represent Ireland in sports].

Places and passions
Well I go a lot to St. Fin Barre's Cathedral, sitting there on my own, and glaring [gazing] at the sky, and that's the best place for me, like, to go sit down. It's a nice garden in the back, which is very old, very wild as well, it's not very well looked after, but I kind like places like that. Going down the river towards the docks, you know, and the way to relax is finding the kind of very remote places so I can be on my own with my thoughts. Insert pic 036 of

My passion in life: it's my occupation, being a musician. Another passion is just teaching music, having music workshops and working with kids and disadvantaged kids, travellers, homeless, unemployed people. A big passion in life is really passing the knowledge of music. It's no secret there you know, music is for everybody, in all styles. My passion is my occupation and it's my, a way of life really. It's my livelihood. And it's only in Ireland where I was given the opportunity to do so and for which I'm forever very grateful and to take the opportunity to thank everybody who gave me this opportunity to be a musician in Ireland, and to survive as a musician.

A favourite phrase
Well I can say 'love breaks rocks.'

Yossi outside Saint Fin Barre's Cathedral, 2006.

7

First Encounters, Talking Cork

Being a stranger, being somewhere new to you, involves many challenges. Suddenly the orientation of the world is different: the landscape, the culture and modes of interaction, ways of thinking, language and accent. All these things are difficult to navigate; misunderstandings happen, the ground shifts, you get tripped up. But gradually you tap into some of how things work differently, and begin to be able to adopt and play with the local doings and sayings...

First Encounters

Marcus Bale

I grew up in Buenos Aires, the capital city of Argentina, a very big city. I've been in Cork for the last five or six years; before that I was thinking of moving from Argentina to travel, experience living in another place, and I always had this interest in early Irish literature, old text and stories, and the folklore of Ireland. I was attracted to it in quite a strong way. I was going to college in Buenos Aires before coming here [and moved over here to attend university].

When I first arrived in Cork, I ran away, terrified, after being here for four months. It was a first encounter. Six years ago, Cork wasn't like it is now, in the sense that foreigners weren't so common, so basically everybody whom I met was Irish, and all the things I was doing were related to Irish people. It was not like I could find some people of my country that I could talk to and relax with, so basically it was a cultural shock; very, very strong. I moved into a little house with three students, seventeen years old – I was twenty-four then – so they were already quite young for me, and you know the kind of life that students have at that age: they go to the pub every night, drinking a lot, and the house is a mess, and everything is upside down, and things were a bit hostile for me. After a couple of months I said, 'Jesus, I don't want this anymore,' and I flew back with my return ticket, and that was my first impression.

Returning to Cork

I came back thinking, 'OK, now I know what I am going to encounter,' and I was more prepared I suppose; I prepared myself better in many ways with paperwork and bureaucracy.

Marcus aged eleven.

Marcus acting with Sarah
Morrey in the play *By
Name and Nature* by Edward
Coughlan.

I had kept in touch with the few friends that I had made and so when I came back there was a whole safety net and it was much, much better. Before, in my previous experience, I was normally dragged to pubs. When I came back I was much, much better prepared for it, because I knew what was coming. If a friend of mine took me to a pub, I knew that we were going to finish very late, and they would be drunk and I would be drunk as well, and it would be a very uncomfortable situation. I had realised it was the only way to socialise, so I couldn't say no, you know, it was something that everybody who comes to Ireland realises after a while. But in the second time it was much more relaxed and I could actually say no, and it was fine. The good side of that was, when I went to the pub, I really wanted to go. For instance, as soon as I arrived I met a friend and he said, 'OK, lets go to the pub,' and we went to the pub, had a couple of pints, started chatting with a couple of girls that were there. After a while they said to me, 'You just arrived, you're looking for a house, we have a room free for rent.' This was just two days after I arrived and I already had a house. Because I was more relaxed about it, this kind of thing, the friendly side of everything, came out.

When I arrived here I already had a very good level of English, but I had never heard an Irish person speak before, and the accent was kind of tricky you know, very, very, tricky. I had many misunderstandings, and that was a big, big thing for me in the beginning. I had to go to Kerry for two months with work, a place near the gap of Dungloe, pretty much a couple of months after I arrived in Ireland. My sister and my brother-in-law were doing a trip, they came and they visited Ireland, and they came to visit me in Kerry. We were staying in a B & B and we took a cab. We told this person where we were going, and he tried to start a conversation with us. Now the accent of the driver, I couldn't understand a word he was saying at all, at all. And my sister and my brother-in-law speak English very well, but for them this was like Chinese or Japanese, this was something completely impossible to understand. But the thing was, since I was here for a couple of months, I tried to kind of cope on. I remember having this bizarre conversation where I didn't understand what he was saying to me, and he was probably wondering what on earth I was saying, because it didn't make any sense, but I just tried to keep it up, because I didn't want my and my sister and brother-in-law to think that I didn't have a clue what was going on. And for twenty-five minutes I kept talking with this man, and I realised that seventy per cent of the conversation didn't make any sense, you know. But my sister and brother-in-law were very impressed, I have to say.

Avreimi Rot
Well, my first experiences were in the countryside, so I guess the good experiences would be encountering nature: those cliffs on the shoreline, and the Atlantic Sea, and the green everywhere, and the trees. You know, people here have forgotten it, but coming from Israel where you have to irrigate everything, seeing all this green and cows everywhere was amazing.

B. O'D.
I remember the third day in Cork I said, 'I'm going to town now and I'm going to find my way home.' So I wasn't sure about the two rivers [the river Lee flows through the city in two channels], I kind of knew about it. It only took me about three hours, and I said,

'I'm not going to ask anybody, I'm just going to find out how to come around this way,' because I always had to ask, and I was sick of it, not to find my orientation. So it took me three hours, and I was going around the North Quay and the south part of the river, God, I'll never forget it. I was going around everywhere, and I got lost around the GPO, and there was a fountain there before, and I said I must get to the fountain again, so I went around in a circle: I was mad.

I couldn't believe it but weather it affected me a hundred per cent. I would never talk about the weather before as much as since I came here. It was raining; I came the end of February, I remember it was raining every day for about two months, and I just couldn't believe it. And then the Summer was very bad that year as well, so I was very, very disappointed with that as well. Actually, you couldn't do anything except be in all the time, that would drive you mad. The weather was depressing, and that was the thing that was totally individual that I couldn't get out. I said, 'How could you people live like this all your life?,' but I actually got a little bit of sun and was all happy then, down to Kerry.

Tony Henderson
Well having no friends really, not knowing very many people, that was the most difficult thing [at the beginning]. The work side of it was hard enough I suppose, but it was just building up a circle of friends and acquaintances really, just that, that's the hardest thing probably anytime when you move to a new place.

Robert Fioure
My first impression of Cork, I remember driving in, I didn't know what to expect. There was a match on when I arrived and the place was very dirty, there was litter everywhere,

Right: Marie-Annick checks her map on the Fever Hospital Steps.

Opposite: Marcus on the day he graduated from UCC with a Bachelor of Arts in Celtic Civilisation and Irish Folklore, 2001.

and we came up MacCurtain Street, and there was a huge amount of litter there. Then I just got a sense, I just thought that Cork looked very interesting: it was very kind of hodge-podge, you know; different colours, different textures, different types of buildings. A lot of the buildings I thought were not looked after like you'd think, very neglected. But it was an interesting town, it was very stimulating because of the different colours, different types of things to see. I noticed that there was only one type of person: it was just Irish people. I'm used to much more, lots of different races and colours and people and that. It was just one type of person, it was white, European kind of people, and very few Africans or darker coloured people, but that has changed in the last five years of course. I do remember thinking it was very mono-cultural.

Marie-Annick Desplanques
The first time that I ever came to Cork, Séamus was working and I was basically exploring the City and getting lost, and lost, and lost because of the bridges. So I went from one bridge to another, and then I walked in the city not knowing where I was. We were living in the Northside at the time, in St. Luke's, and during that first week I looked at the city from the Southside, and I decided, 'Now I am going to walk from Sunday's Well into St. Luke's.' I thought it was going to be uphill, on a [gradual] hill all the time; I didn't realise that there was Blackpool in the middle, so I remember the steps, the famous steps of the old Fever Hospital, because that was the only way to go back up the other side.

Aimée Setter
I originally grew up in London, and I moved over here when I was eight. I moved to the south side in a place called Mahon. Some people would regard it as a rough place, but it can

Lode in Cork in 2005.

be and it can't be: it has its moments like everywhere else. Gangs and violence, drink and drugs, everywhere has it, but that's where I grew up. Well a British person being in Ireland with an English accent, it was hard like, especially when you don't know Irish, and you come over to Ireland, and you have to learn Irish from scratch, and you have to try and figure out what Irish people say, because they speak very fast, so that was a bit hard. But I had some nice teachers, and I made some nice friends, but then you meet the odd horrible person, and it ruins your time here or stays with you, you know. Cork can be a very racist place for you when you are growing up, and you have to either learn to deal with it or get out, and so much so with adults, even people who come over here now, I mean the racist abuse they get is unnatural. It's just something that you have to learn to live with, and not top yourself or anything stupid. I mean if you don't learn to build up a wall against it, you become a very frail person, or a very vulnerable person, there's no point being like that, you just have to get on with it. I think Cork is a lovely place. I mean, any time I travel and come back I say it's nice to be home, because I consider Ireland my home, and I consider Cork my home, probably because I have spent most of my life here, and I have met some lovely people.

Lode Vermeulen
If you are from a big city … I came over here, and it felt like you are driving a car, and you're driving seventy miles, and if you push the brake down, unexpectedly, and you're

going forty miles you know. It was like everything was so slow, everything was so relaxed. I was always so stressed in the Netherlands, because you have to work, you have to study, and it's a fast society. But in Ireland, it was so relaxed, it was nice, it was good.

Talking Cork

Geoffrey D'Souza

Well, 'boy' seems to be the word used in everything: 'How ya, boy? How ya doing, boy? What's happening, boy?,' and the same in the female version, 'How you doing, girl? You OK, girl?' And that is the first thing you would notice, and they just keep shouting it maybe twenty times in a sentence, and everybody you meet on the road they all call you boy, which is very funny you know, but then that is just one of those typical Cork things that people would do. And there is no age barrier, you can be seventy or eighty and it's all the one. Well, the whole thing is that English is like a song to them, they keep singing it in the high notes and low notes, and it's very hard, like: you have to be very, very conversant in the English language to understand what they are talking about.

Emeka Ikebuasi

There is one funny thing that happened. I spoke with someone on the phone, an Irish person, I think that was to the welfare officer or someone. I remember talking to her on the phone and, midway through, or after this discussion, she said to me: 'I'll talk to you later, I'll talk to you later; bye, bye, bye, bye,' and she hung up. So I went back and I stood by my phone, you know? Waiting. [Because] she said she was going to talk to me later, I had in mind she had other things she wanted to talk to me about and that we are not done yet in this issue. So I stayed by my phone, and I just didn't want to go anywhere, and neither did I want to do anything to preoccupy myself when she calls. So I waited throughout the whole day and the call didn't come through, and I wondered, 'why? Is that the way she behaves? Why did she tell me she would talk to me later? I've been waiting all day and her call hasn't come.' And the following day I actually gave her a ring and I said, 'You said to me you were going to talk to me later and I waited all through the day and you didn't ring me up.' And she said, 'No. We're done with our discussion.' And I said, 'But you said that you were going to talk to me later.' She said, 'No, no. That is the usual language here, when we're done with someone on the phone you can always say, "talk to you later, bye, bye, bye".' So I said 'Oh! Now I'm getting into the system.' So that was one funny experience that I had earlier on.

B.O'D.
Cork phrases

'Thanks a million,' 'how bad.' There are thousands of them that I've learned over the years, and I still use them. 'How bad' [used to talk about a positive state of affairs]. What do you mean, 'how bad'? It's not bad, I just didn't get it the first three or four times and then I said, 'just explain it to me, what does it exactly mean?' It's excellent. 'How bad': it's good.

Sometimes the culture and the attitude, I wouldn't understand it. It's easy to understand now. I understand the thinking of Irish people – I'm probably one myself – but I remember, I sometimes found rude the way people were speaking, but then that would be explained by my husband that that's not the way they mean it.

[My experience of settling was] positive because I got to know a lot of people. I was working in a pub when I started, that was positive because I remember after a few months I would know more people and you feel better, you can go anywhere and you would know people to talk to. I think that's the thing about Cork: it's so small. I would never go back to London after Cork, because people are so friendly and you meet so many people, which you wouldn't probably in any other country, because they are so social and they have so many pubs to go to. It's not just about pubs, but there are much more people: you know they make you feel welcome and I think I was the only foreign person, darker looking than the Irish. It was all Irish when I came in here, and maybe that was a bit weird at the beginning, but they totally welcomed me, and they were so nice.

The worst thing about Cork? The worst thing would be probably just … just sometimes Cork can be very cliquey, and that's the worst thing that can happen to anybody you know. I was lucky because I probably see it from a different point of view, as the other half of me, my husband, is Irish. The worst thing would be that some people are really cliquey together and they just don't want to let anybody in, and I know it could happen to anybody, probably if they don't like you they just won't let you in.

Liz Steiner-Scott

It was funny, because in the early days you'd occasionally have experiences, things like getting your chimney swept. I remember ringing up, getting the name off the Echo or something, and ringing up this guy and having this conversation with him on the phone where I couldn't understand a word he was saying and, you know, he must have thought I was from Mars or something. And you'd have funny experiences like that, particularly I found North Cork country accents were tough for me. But I have a very poor ear, as you can hear because I still have an American accent after thirty years, so I obviously am not very good at picking up accents. My husband sounds Irish, people say to me, 'Oh, you married a Cork man.' I say, 'No, I grew up with him you know, he came here as well,' and they don't believe me, because he sounds more Cork. Of course, when I go to the States my parents say to me that I sound very strange, but here everybody says to me, 'Oh, you're on holiday, are you having a good holiday?' Yeah, after thirty years I'm still on holiday!

When I was in hospital, having Charlotte my daughter, in Finbarr's … The first time I was in hospital I was having a threatened miscarriage at twelve weeks, and I had to spend six days on a ward, and I do remember the whole religious thing hit me. At that point when you go into a hospital the first thing they ask you after your name and address is your religion, and I kind of had a hard time getting my head around that, so I took a big deep breath and said I was Jewish, and the woman kind of looked at me strange. Then when I was on the ward I was in the middle bed of one side, in a six-bedded ward. On Sunday morning they came and they curtained me off, and I thought, 'What's going on here?' And you'd be scared back then because I was afraid that I was going to have a miscarriage, and they came in and they put all the curtains around me, and I say to the nurse, 'What's going on?' And then they set up an altar at the end of the ward, and they obviously were going to serve Mass on a Sunday morning. And I said, 'Is there something wrong with me, is there a problem, is the doctor coming, is there something wrong?' 'Oh no,' she said, 'no, no, no, we're just going to have Mass.' And I said, 'So why are you curtaining me off?'

'Oh, we wouldn't think it would be right for you to watch.'

And then the women on the ward, who were lovely women, were all passing around Holy Cards, and of course I thought this was hilarious, and they were passing me over [cards], you know; 'Would you like this one, or would you like this one?' And sticking them into their bras and that kind of stuff you know, and I thought that was very strange and funny.

And then finally when I had Charlotte, she was a very premature baby, and she was in the Special Care Unit in Finbarr's, she wasn't on the bed next to me. I had her in August, and I was up on a farm before that so I was sitting out, and I'm dark skinned anyway, and I had gone very tanned from the summer, And a woman stopped me in the corridor one day, and she said, 'You're the one who had the miracle baby.' I said, 'What do you mean the miracle baby? She was very premature, she was under four pounds, but she's fine.' And she said, 'No, no, no, you're the black woman who had the white baby.' Which amused me.

Robert Fourie

I think the use of language sometimes does lead to misunderstandings between people who have different types of English, like my English is South African English. In South Africa, if you said to somebody, 'Would you ever pass me the salt,' they'd think, 'Oh God, sorry, I didn't realise you wanted the salt.' Saying 'would you ever' would indicate annoyance on your part for them not having realised that you needed the salt. Whereas here 'would you ever' is a very polite way of asking for something, it's just a nice way of saying it. When I first came people would say, 'would you ever do this, would you ever do that,' and I said, 'God, I'm terribly sorry, I didn't realise I was supposed to do that,' so I didn't realise that there was that difference. And then I realised that it was a kind request, whereas instead of making a kind request I'd ask an executive assistant, 'Please type this out.' I would give a direct command, and whereas that would be acceptable in South Africa, it wouldn't be here, and that would put that person's nose out of joint here. So those different ways of using language can lead to misunderstanding, and I think foreigners coming to this country often don't realise that there are different conventions in terms of language use, and that they might be seen as 'bolshy' or whatever, but it's just different customs, different ways of using language and different expectations.

Andy Hawkins
A Corkman in Australia

I got a fierce culture shock when I went there. The first thing that struck me is very peculiar. I'd never - until then - seen adult men wearing short pants and I was fascinated by the fact that people used to go to work in the morning with short pants. But, for the life of me, the Aussies could not understand my accent. I had to speak slow to be understood, and it was very frustrating for me at the time. I could understand these people

Andy on his motorbike,
Perth, Western Australia,
1974.

perfectly well. In the boarding house I had to do my own cooking. The first time I went
to a shop to buy groceries, I walked into the shop and I was asking like I would ask
someone in Cork: 'Could I have bread, sugar, milk,' et cetera. And the woman stood like
a stunned mullet looking at me behind the counter. And then she handed me a pen and
paper. She couldn't understand a word. And I got very frustrated at the time, you see. I
wrote down the list of groceries I needed and I thought, 'I can't go through life like this
in Australia.' Of course I learned to adapt, as you do. I was telling some of the fellows back
in the apartment, and the Scottish man who had been there for years said to me, 'They
can, if they want to, tune into your accent, but some of them just won't.' But at the time
I said, 'Well, they'll have to because this is me. Because I have no problem understanding
them.' And he told me to speak slowly, and I got on famously there.

Marie-Annick Desplanques
The first pub I went into – probably the day I arrived – was the Phoenix and there was a
trad music session. So we were in the pub, and I had a friend from Newfoundland, Peter,

who was there as well, and Séamus and them were playing. At the end the woman of the pub, Monica, she started to scream, 'Would you ever get out,' and I was terrified. Myself and Peter just run out of the pub, and I was saying to Séamus, 'We'll get killed, come on,' and she was screaming, and that must have been the most shocking thing to get people out of pubs that fast and that loudly. I got used to it.

Tony Henderson

I found it difficult to 'get' all sorts of simple things. The pace of life, I suppose the general efficiency I found galling. I had to get used to being told that the plumber would be there at whatever [time] and he wasn't, and there'd be no apology, there would be no follow up, he just wouldn't show up. And you'd phone and they'd say, 'Oh yeah, I'll try get over there tomorrow.' I just wasn't used to that, in fact I never got used to that. I suppose I accept it now as part of the package, because there's kind of a nice side to that as well. I mean there's no point in coming to Ireland and saying, 'We like all these things but we miss the German efficiency.' There's no point in doing that: you take the whole package. But I did, and still do, find that disrespectful, because if you make an appointment with somebody you do it, you are there at the right time, or you make sincere efforts to get in touch with that person and say you can't make it. In any case, that was a thing I found really hard going because it wasn't something that just happened sporadically – it happened a lot, it happened far more than it didn't happen. I remember, early on, I was saying, 'I wonder if I'd be able to make a living here as a furniture maker,' and a friend of mine said, 'Nobody who does what they say they'll do, when they say they'll do it, for the price they'll say they'll do it, will ever be out of work in this country, because you'll have no competition.' And I have found that to be pretty much the case.

Patrícia Manresa

My grandfather was from Cork, and I do believe he had a strong Cork accent. But I remember the first time I heard a strong Cork accent. That was as a child; my uncle in Kerry has a cousin who moved down to live with them, and when I was small I thought she was singing all the time - that she was either singing or complaining. I just did not understand the ups and downs of the Cork accent.

One of the Cork expressions would be, when I used to say things to my cousin in Cork [asking him to do something], he used to always say that he would do them. Like, he would always say, 'I will yeah,' but he never got round to doing them. So it just seemed to me at the time that anything I said was either taken for granted or was dismissed because [from] his answer I assumed that he would do it, and no, I could wait an eternity.

On the bus, any time that I take the bus, and the bus passes in front of a church, people tend to cross themselves, and that is something that struck me, because it's something that people wouldn't do in Barcelona. And people are very polite: even if you bump into someone in Barcelona, there is no such thing as saying, 'I'm sorry,' or, 'excuse me,' you just get on with it; whereas here people would be apologetic, and very kind. They have time for people – people in Cork have time for people, whereas I don't think it would be the same in other cities that I have travelled to.

Dearbhla Kelleher

We have these Cork words and we don't even realise that they're Cork words. 'What's the story, boy,' 'what's the craic.' I remember when we were young, using words like, 'are you going gattin',' you know, bush drinking. My friend now in college with me, she's from Tipperary. Some fellow passed, and I said, 'look at the gatch on him' – you know, the walk on him – and she was looking at me stupid. Some words you wouldn't even notice that you're using like you know, like, 'did you get a bazzer,' a haircut, and we say 'like' a lot as well apparently, she was telling me. 'Like' and 'd'you know' and you don't even realise you'd be using the words, like. We have our own language.

8

Mary O'Sullivan

I grew up in Ballyphehane. I was born in Skibbereen, County Cork, and we moved to Cork when I was about four and a half. And we moved into this little lane, in the Black Ash, in the Kinsale Road, and we had a wagon and a hut. There was this missionary priest, a S.M.A. missionary priest, Father Fennessy, who we still actually have contact with; he at the time would have organised and supported families that moved into that lane to be housed in different areas around Cork. We were one of the families, and we ended up being housed in Ballyphehane, in an estate there.

My mother and father … the decision to settle down was the fact that they had eleven children, and the majority of them would have been young, and I think life on the road was tough. Thinking back now, I would be eternally grateful to them for the fact that they did settle down when they did, because it allowed me to have choices in relation to education. I went to national school and I would have had a very positive experience within that structure.

My mother and father couldn't read and write, so I didn't have that sort of support of going home and saying, you know, 'What's that?' So it actually allowed me to pick things up very fast, and to learn as much as I could. Because I remember I used to actually go into the library at school and bring books home to them, with more pictures than text, because they could understand the story of the picture. It was a huge learning experience for me, and I think that, by bringing stuff home to them, it sort of stayed within my own development and it led to then supporting my own children. And then setting up the homework support group, that was successful because seventy-five per cent of that group would have gone on to second level, they may not have stayed, but they broke the cycle, they went on.

A treat
My mother used to bake cakes, they were called dripping cake, and she used to actually make them with dripping, and she found it awkward in a sense to make them in the house because she was so used to using the outside fire. She often told us they'd actually taste nicer if they were done on the outside fire. If she made them we'd be waiting like, for it to cool off, and you'd cover it then in butter, and you'd sort of go on about your business, out playing or whatever, [with] a big chunk of dripping cake.

Mary being interviewed by the Northside Folklore Project on a field trip to the Barrel Top Project in the National Sculpture Factory in 2004. From left to righ: John Mehegan, Mary O'Sullivan, Marie-Annick Desplanques, Noel O'Shaughnessy and Sean Claffey.

When my mother and father settled down
I could actually see a change in them. They had left something of themselves behind. My father was a tinsmith, and when we moved into the house, he built a little forge thing out the back for his solder iron, and I probably still have scars from holding the soldering thing in the fire for him to do tin work. He used to fix lawn mowers and umbrellas and stuff like that, and people from Ballyphehane now used come and the discussions … as a child you'd be there, and the talks and stories and stuff like that. And then you'd have the situation where older traveller men then would visit him, and like you'd be in the sitting room, they'd go into this mode of, 'Do you remember when?,' you know, and you'd be sitting there listening to all these stories. About when they were busking in the streets in Killarney and, 'Do you remember that big fight with such and such a fella?,' you know, and you'd be goggley-eyed like, and you'd be sitting there listening. Or he used to tell the ghost stories, aw Jesus, he used tell ghost stories and even now I'd tell them to, I used tell 'em to my children, and I'd be getting a shiver. He used to tell us the ghost stories and I swear to God it would frighten the life out of us, we used to be going up to bed then, up the stairs and, like, grabbing on to each other's nightdresses and sort of running up the stairs together.

He used to sing one song, 'O'Sullivan John to the Road You've Gone,' I can remember him singing it. Pecker Dunne, who is an older traveller man now, he would have busked with my father now years ago. He'd have his bodhrán and his songs, and my father would have the melodeon and they'd just take off … Kerry and West Cork.

My older sister, Hanny, years ago, she used sell swag, which the majority of traveller women used do, years ago. They had a basket and they'd have all these little holy relics and medals and stuff like that, paper flowers and things. And they go through the villages, and sell 'em. And I went with Hanny, I was about eleven I'd say and she was going back to Kerry now, to link up with Nonie Harrington and Dinny and the people that were actually travelling. And at that time they were travelling around they would have been living in tents.

I remember that we were staying in a little place outside Kenmare and Dinny and Nonie, now, had their tent pitched and then Michael Coffey and his wife had their tent pitched there. Hanny's van was here and we were sleeping in the back of that. We were outside a sort of a manor, no one lived there, it was sort of gone desolated. And they built an outside fire and I loved this, like. Nonie would have done her bacon, cabbage and spuds on the fire you know, and I had that, and I was going, 'Oh, this is brilliant.' And Dinny then started with his stories, oh my God, I'll never forget it. Lady Palmer, now we were outside the gate of this Lady Palmer's house, right, and we were sitting around an outside fire, complete darkness all around us, and he started this story about the dog monster that was … she had a big huge garden, big huge garden. He said, 'Look in over the wall there now,' to the children that were there. So we got up and we were sort of looking in, he said, 'Can ye see the big boulder that's in there?' And we said, 'Yeah, yeah, it's over there,' and he said, 'That's where he's buried.' Well I swear to God, I got weak, I can remember running screaming to Hanny and she was there, she was saying, 'Would you stop it, he's only messing,' and I was going, 'It's in there, he's under it, oh Jesus Christ, I'm going to bed.' But like, that was the ideal time to tell a story like that, outside, at an outside fire, with complete pitch blackness all around you. And of course he was laughing like, 'cause us children, we were screaming, we were saying, 'Oh, we don't want to hear no more, no, no, don't tell us.' 'He's in there now and it's known, it's a common thing in Kenmare, that people see him, in the w…' Well, I didn't sleep; I did not sleep that night.

Cork phrases

You say something to someone and she says, 'I will, yeah,' but that means, 'No, go away,' but they're saying 'I will, yeah.' I laugh at that. Even my own daughters, now, because they're from Cork, you'd go and say, 'Oh, will you do something there now?,' and I get sometimes, 'I will, yeah.' That is what sticks in my head about the Cork accent. And going down the Coal Quay, I love going down there and listening to people. If you're looking at something on the stall, and just sort of having that quick conversation with the woman on the stall about nothing, that sort of thing now.

I am a citizen of Cork

It's also part and parcel of Cork as well because I am … I am a citizen of Cork, and when I go away outside of Cork, we'll say to a conference in Germany or America, and they say, 'Where are you from?,' I'd be saying 'Cork.' I mean you nearly forget to say Ireland. And they say, 'Where's that?' 'Oh that's in Ireland, I'm from Cork.' But you know it's that

Mary in Cork, 2005.

sense of being from a specific place. We would have moved from the site to England, years ago, we moved to live there. And I just remember, like, I was… I couldn't settle. And then I was saying, 'Oh God, that's probably a traveller thing now,' but I was not happy until I got … We decided after six months, 'No, we're going back to Cork,' and I remember like, the sense of relief. There was this thing that was there, and I didn't know it, but I sensed it when I actually got back off the boat, back here, in Cork, back to the site. I just let out a sigh of relief that I was back. I remember feeling that sense of belonging coming home, and I remember saying it to my husband and he was saying like, 'Yeah, you know, we won't be moving out of here again.'

Describe Cork in three words.
Lively, colourful and em … a sense of richness that I haven't experienced anywhere else.

9

Here, There and In-between

When you're in a foreign country that has become your home, how do you keep links with ways of speaking, eating, celebrating, being, that are part of the other home, the one you have left, while exploring a new way of living? And what about the generations to come? This chapter explores some of how people mediate the inexorable melding with Ireland through everyday life and the desire to keep in touch with what shaped them up to this.

Lode Vermeulen

There is a Dutch community [club]. They have several meetings a year. I'm not a member of that club, I don't know why, but I was there last year. We have 'Queen's Day' in the Netherlands, that was the birthday of the Queen, but she died. But we're still celebrating that day, the birthday. So it's a big tradition, it's a big party in the Netherlands: the thirtieth of April. My colleague, he organised a party with the Dutch community, and it was in the Heineken brewery in Cork. I came there, I saw different kinds of people, some of them were retired, some of them are quite young, some of them, they were engaged or married with Irish women. I spoke to a Dutch man who couldn't even talk Dutch anymore, because he was married with an Irish woman, so it was very funny to see that.

Emeka Ikebuasi

Usually, when I go out socialising … there was a club that used to accommodate us on Sundays - that's at Sullivan's Quay - the Christian Brothers' School. A lot of us who were members of the St. Vincent de Paul, usually we congregate there on Sundays after church service. Some people can play tennis, some maybe play dance music or basketball, football … a little space that can accommodate all that. And then people have their coffee and tea and biscuits. And other places I usually can go out socialising is the African restaurant, which is on MacCurtain Street, the Eko Restaurant. They serve all sorts of African and the Caribbean foods. The South Africans go up there to patronize the place, you have the Caribbeans, the Congolese, the Nigerians, the Togolese, the Zimbabweans, the Kenyans, the Chadians, the Rwandans … a lot of them who are up there. There's also a new place, in Blackpool, which is the Afrobar. And a lot of us, you know blacks, or the minorities go up there and the locals also, and we go out to have a good time. [The English language] is usually an easier way for us to communicate amongst ourselves because the French-speaking Africans, they also know the broken English, and the English-

Chuky Dandy foodstore with the
shopkeeper waiting to start work.

speaking Africans also speak the broken tongue, for us to interact, to get to talk to each
other.

But up in Carrigaline, at times I go to the … there is a notable bar that they say has been
there for ages, Rosie's Bar. I've been there a couple of times. I'm not a drinker, I don't
actually drink but I just go there to … sit by. Because a friend of mine, you know, I have
a lot of friends who would ask me out; and definitely it's an opportunity for me to get to
talk and know the people better.

Vitaliy Mahknanov
The Eastern European community at the present moment are, if you look at the statistics,
two thousand in Cork. There were only five hundred families, but in the present moment
[2004] for two years, the figure has probably increased. In February of this year we
established an Eastern European Association in Ireland, and in our first annual meeting
there were about seventy people, but we didn't do any advertisement, everything come
from word of mouth. But in Cork we can find Eastern European products in shops as
well, on the North Main Street.

I want to prepare a radio programme in the Russian language that would be possible,
for half an hour once a week, especially for children. There are a lot of children who
were born here and some of the children who are already teenagers, they are losing their
language skills, and for that it would be very handy to have some programme, something

The Eastern European shop, Old Russia, on North Main Street.

they can listen to on a daily basis. Maybe a pilot version for a couple of weeks, do the program for half and hour, and afterwards something more concrete.

Isabelle Sheridan

There's a big [French] community actually, it got really big in the past three to four years, very big because of all the call centres around. When I arrived it wasn't such a big community, it was still good size enough, but people knew each other a lot more. Now there are an awful lot more people that you wouldn't know, and I am kind of part of the old people you know, I have children here and all this, so I don't meet the younger people systematically. There is a group for children: that was started probably six or seven years ago. And so we meet every Friday night in Togher - in l'Arche - so they have activities and you know it's not school really, it's just activities for the children. Some of them have been enrolled to give them contact with other kids in a different language, because sometimes if you have children and you speak French to them during the day you are the only adult they speak French to, and after that they speak to all their friends in English and obviously they don't speak French with other children, so we've been trying to do that. And there's also a library for French kids, was opened actually by the Ambassador last May in Tigh Filí - it's a friend of mine Sophie who runs it; she has a bookshop as well, books in different languages, so you can go there and borrow a book as well. It's open to everybody: it's not only for French you know, but it's all French books, you know children's books. And

Geoffrey at the The Four Liars restaurant where he works as a chef.

then there's my stall [in the English Market], which is also a bit of a social contact: a lot of French people come to the English market to get good food.

Adam Skotarczak
There are a lot of Polish people here. We meet from time to time with our friends, we go to pubs or clubs, have good fun. The Irish accent is sometimes difficult. It depends. I was talking to one man, it was easy for me to understand him, but sometimes I meet different people, and they talking with different accent, and sometime it's really hard to understand them. Sometimes I must ask people to say again three or four times, because of that. [I have] a lot of misunderstandings, but every day it's easier for me. All the people, when I met them, they say, 'Hello how are you?' I say, 'I'm OK, and yourself?' [because] this is what I hear when I first came here. 'And yourself': it is real Cork, it's real nice. There's not something like this in England, in Ireland only, I think.

Keeping in contact with family in Poland
I send some email by internet; I call my family. I call my home every week. I talk to my mother, with my sisters, sometimes I call to my friends, and I talk to them. I spent Christmas with my family, I was one week in Poland for Christmas. At first it was really nice to be with my family because I haven't seen them for half a year. It was really good to see my sisters, and my mother, my parents, and to be with my friends.

Marcus Bale

Yes, there is a community from South America here now. Maybe two years ago I would say no, but now I would say yes, and you can see it constantly because there are certain pubs and places where these people meet. And now you can learn how to dance Tango and Salsa in Cork, and how to do Capoera or Samba, which are Brazilian. There are South American movies coming into Kino more often than before; there's food that you can start finding that you couldn't find before; there's quite a big community of people from South America in general.

Karina Abdoulbaneeva

[A treat for my children would be] going to visit their grandparents in Russia, that's what they really enjoy. But, like, in two or three weeks' time they ask me, 'Mam, when we are we going back home to Cork?'

Geoffrey D'Souza

Sure, I don't cook a bit of Indian food at all. I was cooking European food back in Goa as well. I wouldn't be a good expert of traditional Cork things, like I wouldn't be making drisheen or tripe or anything. You learn a lot as well when you come over, what do people like, you know like. You would learn to make colcannon, you learn to make mash Irish style with the green onions thrown in. [Seeing a Kerry mother cooking] those are the things you remember, you know: you have a roast leg of lamb; they get rosemary from the garden; the gravy is made in the pan, you know; the roast potatoes are roasted in the tin; you watch and learn, and those are fantastic experiences. You have more of an interaction in a real sense that you know what are you learning.

Robert Fourie

I'm here nearly five years, and I do feel when I talk about things I am now unconsciously talking about *us*, when I talk about Irish people. I used to talk about, 'you Irish people, you guys' … When I first came I felt very alien, I did feel alien, and it took a long time to understand how Irish culture works. It's very different to where I come from: people here are not direct: they are indirect, they are subtle people, they are very witty people, they value verbal skills very much, and you can't be direct. People are very polite, they don't value directness, people don't like being confronted, whereas in South Africa, you tolerate that, it's part of life, people are very confrontative in South Africa. And so I had to learn to be less direct, and to tone myself down a little bit with people, and not just say, 'well, no, I don't like that,' or, 'would you stop doing that,' because my natural inclination, if somebody is annoying me, I would say, 'would you ever stop doing that now.' I wouldn't make a comment like that now, do you know. [If there's a problem with, for example, someone making too much noise at work,] Irish people tend to make some kind of martyred statement that, 'The noise levels are really rising in the office these days,' instead of just telling the person, 'Shut up, I'm trying to work,' they make some oblique comment. And I had to learn that, I still make mistakes that way, I still tell somebody what I think of them, and people don't like that, but I do find that I am adjusting to the culture of Ireland and Irish people. I talk about the political policies of the government or whatever,

Robert showing a friend from South Africa around Cork, pictured here outside the Old Cork Gaol.

and I talk about *us* when I am talking about Irish people. I found myself doing that more and more, I am feeling more that I am part of ... I am starting to feel Irish a little bit, although I am very South African.

I feel happy here, I feel I'm part of the furniture now. But it's taken a long time – it's not easy to make friends in Cork: it is a bit cliquish, people don't make a lot of effort to include you in their circles, it's easy to be left out. I don't think that is particular to Cork, I think that is particular to any country where you are a foreigner, and I still feel like a foreigner sometimes, but I'm feeling less and less like that. I think the effort also comes from myself, like, you make the effort to be included in things. I do think that sometimes Irish people are not used to foreign people yet, they are very mono-cultural still, and I think that as time goes by, people will realise more and more that the foreigners also need to be looked after a little bit, because we *do* contribute to the society and we *do* add value to the society. I think sometimes foreigners get left out of social circles, and that kind of ... I sometimes get lonely here as well, I sometimes feel quite lonely, and you know that could be ... that is part of my own self, but also because I don't have a family here, I don't have my sisters, my brothers, my aunts, uncle ...

10

Vitaliy Mahknanov

I grew up in the largest city in western part of Ukraine, L'viv. In English it would be, 'City of the Lion.' It was established around the twelfth century, as a fortress that protected the western part of the country from Mongol invasion. It became a big city, which has about seven circles of protection walls. Well, I grew up in the city centre, from that time when Ukraine was part of USSR and the city became more modernised. That part where I used to live was the outskirts of the city, but when it became an industrial city it was exactly the city centre. So I had access to everywhere only for one, two minutes of walking. The population would be about one million.

When I was young I liked to play with all my friends and feel myself as a part of the society, I had the feeling, if a friend is near by then if something happens to you, somebody is able to help you. And I enjoyed sport, if you just ask me any type of sport that I didn't do, it's probably would be difficult to me answer. I tried almost everything. When you are a kid, everything is the same to you as a big sun-shiny day, your parents around you, everything is fine, you have your sweets and you don't think about the future. But when you grow up and one day find yourself alone, I'm already adult and I have to do something, life becomes a bit more difficult and a different perspective opens for you, and it brings new changes into your life as well.

I grew up in a family, which would be, compared to an Irish family, a little family. My mum was third of four children and I remember the big celebrity [celebration] when my grandma had a birthday and all the family came together with grandparents, grandchildren and children, and all together about twenty people celebrating grandma's birthday. I have a little brother and mum and my stepfather, 'cause when I was kid my father died. He was a vet, and I wanted to follow his direction. I wanted to become a surgeon or solicitor, because I wanted to help people in a practical way, but after that I found, when I finished school, it was quite an expensive education [for that], and I became a journalist, and I'm really happy about the things I did. The doctor helps people to recover from illness, but the writer, he solves with interesting thoughts, interesting ideas that people can read through later on, maybe they can discover something for themselves or understand reality better than before. Doctor would be more practical way to help people: a writer, a journalist would be on a deeper level, like a counsellor or whatever.

Arriving in Cork

I arrived in 2002. I spent couple of weeks in Dublin, later came to Cork. And in the beginning for me it was a quite different understanding of reality, because I found a very dark and very low sky. It was December and everything was grey, and brought me to depression. It was a new world, and all your life left behind, and you have to see something new in your life. And the same time I was very amazed with the fresh air and very dark sky, with the stars, it's almost the same as in Ukraine, it reminds me of my home. So that would be my first experience when I arrived in Cork, and I felt myself quite, how do you say, not comfortable.

First impressions

From outside, [it's] all about the architecture and all the physical things you can see on your way. And inside would be about your style of living, and this community, who you involve with, and just everyday people you meet. Cork is rebuilding a lot of buildings everywhere - compared to Ukraine it was something unusual that we have so big and extreme building everywhere - every corner of the city there are building sites. For me it was like understanding that life here has a big future and big potential because everything is growing up and developing, compared to now we can see there's a lot of things done, lots of new buildings, renovation done. Patrick's Street is already almost finished. So when I saw it for the first time, for myself it would be something scary at the beginning, at the same time you can understand the big progress going on, the city developing and just growing up.

[That's the] external side of understanding of the city, but internal would be my relation with the people and I felt myself in a big frustration. First of all for me was language barrier, because English is not my mother language. If you compare my level today with two years ago, you would be laughing at me and saying, 'OK, come on, stop it, say again, repeat, I don't understand.' And the second problem for me was [at] those time, sources of information; How can I survive? Who can I go to? Where can I get information? And what is perspective in life, for me, for the future? It's still the same problem, because I cannot find exactly the proper way, decent way, how can you see your future clearly? Unless you are a native Irish person, or unless you were born here, you have much more difficulties, to get used to those style of living, because I would say [there] would be big difference in culture, if you compare Ukrainian culture and Irish culture. But at [the same] time there would be a lot of relevant and similar points of both cultures.

A good experience, I remember one of the best, it was when my daughter was born. I found myself very happy that time to become a father, it was a new title for myself and I began to feel myself more responsible. For you're already a man who has a kid and he has to look after that, not only your wife, but also your kid. I think much harder, not one step in front, several steps in front, to go in the proper way and see something in the future. And at the same time I found new people who became my friends here in Ireland, a French guy and his Irish girlfriend, she used to work in media and radio as well. So for me it was big positive thing because before I felt myself like a lonely person, who has only family, and I reminded myself of the big celebration of life. I mean that life that I had behind me was something bright and interesting, but since I became a Cork citizen, for me everything was quite different. I couldn't understand myself, where I'm going, how can I survive, what can I do. It was a big time of pressure, and depression as well. But the best thing was the birth of my daughter and my first friends that I found in this country.

In Slavic languages we use the words 'thank you,' and, 'please,' but ordinarily, we use intonation to say something. And by intonation it can just show what you mean. But in the English language you have to put this small word 'please' everywhere. Unless you do this people treat you in a different way. I mean, if you go to the shop and say, 'Can I have this?,' and forget to say 'please,' people are watching you very strangely, throw it on the table, and so on. But later on you presume, 'What's wrong with me, what did I do wrong?' Try to rewind your sentence back a sec.: 'Ah, sorry, I forgot to say the word, "please."' And, next time when you start to learn from this thing, and you start to say it in beginning: 'Please can you tell me, or give me something?' Rather than in our language, where we do everything by intonation mostly in [these] situations.

People will be more direct in Ukraine, I would say. If people like you, they would say like, 'Well, I like you because you are nice person, because you are always coming in time, because you are reliable, because something between us is very close.' Or, if a person met you for the first time, they can tell you, 'Sorry, I don't like you, better just stay away and not head my direction,' but not ignoring you. Ireland would be different, people will smile at you, I call this myself, hypocrisy, but maybe it's part of the culture, I don't know. People say, 'Oh yeah, it's cool, give you ring tomorrow, no worries boy. Come on, I'll take you tomorrow [and so on].' But then, nothing happens, [and you think], 'What's wrong with me, maybe I misunderstood because of my English problem.' Day by day you come across this thing, not once, twice, a couple of times, you come to understand this part of the

Left: At the Lough with his children Emilia and Vladimer.

Below: A Christmas party with friends and family.

Opposite: Vitaliy, his wife Orlena and daughter Emilia.

culture and people. Another proverb says: 'In Rome do as the Romans do.' For me it's a big deal now: I try to get involved in Irish culture, Irish society, as much as possible, but I want to save my identity and feel myself as I am in my present form.

On going out

Ah well, you see, while you're a married person and have big responsibility, you don't get used to hanging out. A friend of mine, he showed me different parts of Cork. I found there are too many pubs in Cork. On every single corner: it's again part of the culture. And one of those pubs I really like; the Franciscan Well. It's a local brewery and it's very nice beer over there. And another friend of mine, my English teacher, Michael, he showed me another pub, Charlie's, and he said, 'In this pub you can see traditional music, and meet average people, all kinds of people who exist in the in the city.' Another place I like is the Bodega bar, you feel very comfortable [there]. Quite often you see people, not only Irish, from different countries, they mix together in that place and you feel yourself quite comfortable.

Humour

Sometimes the Ukrainian humour takes advantage of other countries but not always. For example, one anecdote, a Ukrainian woman married a foreigner, and at first they [have a] conversation, with the man trying to explain to the wife:

'Look, when I came home and you see my hat on the back of my head, I will be happy, I will love you all night, but if I come home and the hat is in the front of my eyes, I'm very angry: don't touch me and leave me alone.'

His wife looked at him and said:

'Listen dear, when you come home and see me with arms towards to you, it means you are welcome, I will feed you, I will love you all night. But if you come home and you see me standing with my hands on my hips, it means I don't care where your hat is!'

A request for the Irish people
I have one wish for the Irish people. I mean request, maybe, I don't know the particular word to describe what I mean, it's maybe a complex thing. First of all, I want to ask them to be more respectful and polite to the foreigners who exist in this country. And maybe, maybe I have no right to say this, to spend less money on drinks, but more money for self-education. I mean later on people might, might understand more about life, more about the perspective of having somebody close to you, who you can talk to. And the last thing is to say an anecdote to make it more funny. I'm thinking how I can translate this thing, you know, because it's very difficult, sometimes when you interpreting the joke it's losing its sense.

Two fishermen are going fishing. and they call to another man passing by, 'Hey, Vucov, are you coming today, are you going tomorrow, for fishing?'

And that person says, 'No.'

They say, 'Why don't you go fishing?' And he says:

'Because my wife, she allows me to drink vodka at home.'

11

The City

The city seen through different eyes…

Liz Steiner-Scott

In the early days people would say, 'what do you miss from America?' And we used to laugh because [it's] little things like bagels, which now you can get here, silly things like that. I buy *matzoh* when I see it in the market. It's the unleavened bread. It's like a cracker, and for a while you could get in the supermarket, which was great. I just like it; it happens to be Jewish food. I buy it now at one of the stalls in the [Old English] market.

I shop there every Saturday morning. [The change there has been] huge. Do you remember when it burned? And they redid it, and it really came up, and it's fantastic, I think it's the best thing going in Cork city. It's what makes Cork really unique; I love it on a Saturday morning, and I love going in and doing bits and pieces, and then having a coffee at Mary Rose's. It's just nice, and you meet people and you see everybody. Ten o'clock on a Saturday morning: I love that.

I spent a semester teaching in America in 1994, and I really missed Cork on a Saturday morning. I couldn't believe how much I missed it. I'd get up on a Saturday morning in this little tiny town in Maine and it was so, like, there was nothing to do, and I felt at loose ends, I didn't know what to do with myself. Even wandering into a bookshop, wandering into the Market, just having a poke around, I missed that. So I realised how much I really do rely on the centre of town.

Billy McCarthy

The Lough in Cork comes to mind straightaway – the earliest memories I have of going someplace without my parents. It would be fifteen, twenty minutes walk from where I lived in Quaker Road. We used to go there after school to fish for torneens, sticklebacks and roach and rudd; long summer evenings fishing for those.

My brother had a what we would call a 'racing bicycle,' a bicycle with turned down handlebars, and he was very, very particular about that: he wouldn't let us use that, we were too young, and that was his pride and joy. But one summer he went to the country working as a helper on a combine harvester - combine harvesters were very new at the time, and they used to require so many people working around them - and he was doing that for the whole summer, and while he was away I took advantage of his bike. One day

Left: The Old English Market.

Below: Moynihans Poultry in the market.

Billy by the Lough, 2006.

we were cycling in the Lough. Now, you can walk right around the Lough: there is an inner path and an outer path; the outer path was always regarded as an 'Irish mile,' it would take a person walking a good ten minutes to walk it. That wasn't good enough for me: I was cycling the bike in the inner path. Now there is a little wall all the way around it, it is about ten inches high, and while I was cycling around the Angelus bell rang. The Angelus bell rang, and being brought up in the strict religious code that I was, I made a Sign of the Cross, and to do that of course it entailed taking my right hand off the handlebar, and while I had lost concentration for that moment, the front wheel of the bike struck the curb which ran right around the Lough, and I went head over heels *into* the Lough with the bicycle following on top of me. Completely submerged in the water, and that's the way I had to go home and confess my sins, that I had taken my brother's bike out and that I had to suffer the consequences. That for me was the Lough: it has many, many memories, and I brought my children there down the years, and now I bring my grandchildren there.

Fitzgerald's Park

Fitzgerald's Park, too, was obviously a great attraction for us young people, particularly in our teenage years, when guys like myself were chasing the girls. You were always bound to find them around Fitzgerald's Park lying out there in the sunshine, and I think that is

Isabelle Sheridan.

where we did most of our courting in our time. A lot of memories too in the Marina
for the same reason; you know we didn't have any transport or anything like that, so all
these places were in walking distance and we would spend many, many hours around
there. All those things, they all mean something, and they're all memories of childhood
and growing up in Cork.

Isabelle Sheridan
I never meant to take a stall in the Market
In '92 the English Market wasn't the way it is now, it was getting not a very good reputation
in Cork, and the stalls had been let down a bit, there were loads of empty stalls and nobody
wanted them. And then year by year it improved, and the market is now running so well,
it is so bright and there is a diversity of products, and still what makes it very special is the
mixing of old and new, you see. You meet so many people who actually have memories of
the market when it was at its best, at the time it was a very big place in Cork city.

Isabelle's stall, On the Pig's Back
I wanted a name with pigs in it because *charcuterie* means pork, and I wanted an Irish name
because I'm French but I live in Ireland, and I'm also Irish even if I'll never be totally
Irish and I'll never be French again, do you know what I'm saying? And because the stall
is for Irish people, not just French people and tourists. So I asked my husband and he
said, 'On the pig's back,' and I still couldn't say it in Irish then, *ar mhuin na muice*. And we
have lovely bags, with *On the Pig's Back* on them, you see them everywhere now, even
in Dublin. I had a customer who was living half of the year in Italy and half the year in
Cork, and he said, 'Isabelle, you won't believe what happened. I was in Rome sitting in

On the Pig's Back, the Old
English Market.

the terrace in a café, and what did I see passing by, only somebody with an *On the Pig's Back* bag on them, and I felt like at home.' And it was the best compliment I could get, it was really nice, to feel at home because you see a bag from the market.

It's a very central part of the city alright, and it's lovely to see it now moving up and getting new people, and you want new people and old people. That's actually the secret: everywhere else in Ireland now they're trying to do markets, and you know in Dublin they're trying to revive some of their markets that they had before, but nothing comes up to this one because of the mixing of the old and the new. Like, you go to the butcher here and he'd be advising you and all this: everybody will give you a recipe if you go to the market. I seem to be meeting loads of people who are actually related to people who had stalls in the market. A lady came to me and said, 'My granddad used to have your stall where you are here.' And they were small stalls, family stalls, and some people are there for three generations. There's a lot of history; that's what makes it very special.

Tim O'Brien
What does Cork mean to me?
God, that's a big one. The words of the song, *My Home By The Lee*. Do you know, there's an awful lot in the place; this is where I feel most comfortable. I've done a fair bit of travelling in my life, but when I walk down the streets of Cork I just … I've a history of

Left: Father Mathew.

Opposite: Charlie's Bar, Union Quay.

association with the place, I know the place. I knew it before it changed, I knew what it was like before. So I suppose it's just a feeling of belonging that everything is more or less familiar about the place, do you know?

I remember as a young fella going to school: when you were finished school in the Mon, about four o'clock in the evening, the fashion was you would troop down for town, and then you would flagwall Pana. You would go down one side and up the other, and then you would be very busy looking out to see who you would see. That was a tradition. And then you'd stop by Eason's and if you spotted someone that you wanted to spot, and they kept going, then you would kind of go off, and you would walk with their group until you got a conversation going or whatever. But that was a tradition: Pana, up one side and down the other. Now it's like Pana's a parking place for taxis – there's nothing moving up or down there. They have these streetlights around the place that you would split yourself on if you're not watching the whole time, so I think they actually destroyed it.

Now the statue of Father Mathew just on the bridge.
You know his hands are like that, [as if to say], 'up there they're drinking since they were that high,' so that was why he brought the Pioneer thing to Cork, well that was the joke of it anyway. And behind him there was this busman's shelter, well that wasn't a busman's shelter at all, that was a fireman's shelter. They used to keep a ladder on wheels over there with buckets, they had two firemen sitting in it, and when someone would run down to Pana to say that there was a fire, the boys would get out their ladders and their wheels, and the buckets and they would get some other fellas and they would push the ladder

up, and the buckets would go for water, and the ladder would be thrown up against the building to get the people out. And that's what it was there for.

Rob Stafford
The things that I like about Cork city
Charlie's session on a Sunday. I like the Cork School of Music. I think it's great, the fact that you've got a small town with brilliant classical music as well as traditional music, and then there's all different types of music here, and a very high standard for such a small place. That's what I find quite unusual about Cork, particularly the School of Music to have such a high standard in a small town.

Patrícia Manresa
What makes Cork Cork? Well I must say that I started understanding Cork when I realised that the Lee was divided. Like, the Lee would be a big landmark to me, because when I first walked round the city, and I'm usually quite good in cities, I just couldn't figure the city out. And then when I realised that there was a split in the river, that was when I made Cork mine, and I understood the city.

I used to live in Adelaide Street, which is just off North Main Street. One of my main priorities when I arrived in Cork and was looking for a place, was that I just had to live in the city centre. I suppose I still needed that buzz, that I had in Barcelona, of being anonymous. My flatmates were really nice, and I owe my staying in Cork to them really. I remember my flatmate – they were all from Cork – saying, 'You'll know if someone likes you if they slag you off.' And I couldn't understand that at first, but it seems to be recurrent behaviour in Cork, that when somebody slags you off, it means that they like you, which is good. It's good for me to know anyway so I don't take it personally.

My mother is from Ireland. We used to always go in summertime to my uncle in Kerry. We used to arrive on the ferry to Cork, so Cork was the first city that I saw when arriving to Ireland, and one of the memories I have is of the coloured houses: when I saw the houses painted all different colours, I knew that I was in Ireland. And just that sense of relief, and of joy of seeing my family again, and just being in Ireland, because that meant a holiday for a whole month and having a great time. I remember my mother . . . when we were driving past what used to be a mental hospital before [Our Lady's hospital], I don't know what that is now, but my mother used to say, 'that's the longest building in Ireland.' And any time I heard those words I knew that we were travelling down to Kerry and we were leaving Cork behind.

My idea of Cork has changed, there's a sense of Cork being familiar to me now, it's a part of my life now. When I was a child, it was only a city that I passed through as opposed to a city that I made my own, and I have made Cork my own now.

Stefan Wulff
I find the Marina very interesting. I'm into rowing myself, I row currachs [traditional canvas-covered canoes] with a club, Naomhóga Chorcaí. The Marina's a great place to launch boats, and to have the choice either going down to Blackrock, or going up to the city, and certainly the city is an interesting place to row into. We have a choice of going two ways [into the city]: either we take the South Channel or we take the North Channel. Going the South Channel, depending on the tide, you might get as far as the Meitheal Mara building at Crosses Green itself. Going into the North Channel you pass by Merchant's Quay, and it's a very busy area, and people would notice us, and they'd look or they'd comment in certain ways.

A couple of months ago we were rowing up the North Channel to the Mercy Hospital, and at the bridge in front of the North Gate Cinema there were three women who kind of were calling us and waving. We thought they were just excited to see us, and they said, 'Can you come over here, we just dropped something.' They were laughing all the time, and I thought they were having us on, but anyway we went over there, and they said, 'We dropped money in there, we dropped a fifty Euro note.' We said, 'Get out of it,' but it was true, it was floating there. There was a strong tide going down, and so it took quite a bit of manoeuvring to get close enough to the fifty Euro note, so but eventually we got it, and I climbed up one of the ladders that you can see along the quay to pass it on. The woman who had lost it said, 'Look, I have ten Euros here for you,' and I said, 'It's all right, it was our pleasure really to get involved in this rather unusual event.'

Cork seen from a currach
It depends on the weather on the day and the level of the tide: if it's very low you look a lot at the quay walls. If it's high, you can see quite a bit of city life, which in itself can be very interesting; just to see how people move, and the way they might talk to each other, just to see street life. If you have the right light, if it's coming towards the cooler season

Stefan, left, in a currach at Bachelor's Quay with other Naomhóga Chorcaí members.

and you have a nice dry day, the sun is shining, blue sky, I find it amazing, really smashing, you know the way the buildings come across. There's this intense light, and they might glow kind of golden. Everything seems so much more detailed and intense, quite often I take my camera and take shots, and it's extremely worthwhile to experience Cork from that perspective. To go underneath bridges, take a look back, take a shot with the camera, and to really get a different impression of the city.

Brigid Carmody
Well where we live here, it's the only group housing scheme in Cork for travellers. There are seven families living here. They're all related, so it's a very safe place for the kids. I have four kids now and when they come back from school they just go out, they're always close, they never go on the road, there's always someone to watch them and it's handy, if you run out of milk or sugar, you just hop over the wall. Or if you're short a babysitter, there's always someone here, so it's very secure here.

I like Patrick's Street, everything you need is there. Once you go in, you can just park and get everything in one place. [For a tour of the city] where would I start off? Fitzgerald's Park: the museum, or just going out to the park just for the day, I take the kids out to Fitzgerald's Park regularly now, just for the day, to go on the swings and kick a ball around and things like that. I can remember going there as a child on school tours, and I can remember thinking they hadn't anything relating to travellers. We'll have the Barrel Top Wagon out there soon: that'll be a big thing [for the children], to actually go in and see part of their culture in the museum, which will be brilliant. It's a Cork Traveller Women's Network Project: there are two traveller men and one tutor working, building the Barrel Top wagon, and it's just coming to the final stages now. We're just starting to prepare for the launch and are getting ready for the move to Fitzgerald's Park.

I like the fountain [on the Grand Parade], because that was always there, it hasn't been changed, you know. And, I remember going out, as a teenager, that's where we'd meet up. We'd all meet at the fountain and we'd head off then to the disco or the bars. Whichever one we got into, we were usually thrown out of them like, but …

[We'd go to] Chandra's, which is the Grand Parade hotel, I think. It's just there by the fountain, we used to try there but the bouncer would never let us in. We'd spend two hours getting ready and get someone to drop us in town, and go to a bar for a couple of drinks and then try a couple of clubs. We might try five and get into one, but we would spend a lot of time walking around trying to get into clubs. It was terrible because there'd be a line of people either behind you or in front of you, and you'd be waiting your turn and when we'd get right to the bouncer he'd say to you; 'No, I don't want your kind in here.' And you'd turn around, and everyone is looking at you and wondering what 'your kind' is, you know what I mean. You'd just have to hang your head and walk away, there is nothing you can do about it, you just have to walk away, so it is a terrible feeling. But as young girls we'd just keep going back, and keep trying and trying and trying, and hope that was a different bouncer on the night, and that we'd get in somewhere.

Mahbub Akhter
When I first arrived in Ireland, I came to Shannon, and I found it very, very quiet, and the whole place looked completely empty. From the plane I saw the square fields very much green like home, but so, so empty. Bangladesh is a very, very crowded country:

Right: Examining the Barrel Top Wagon in the National Sculpture Factory shortly after its completion in 2005.

Opposite: Our Lady's Hospital, now converted to apartments.

we have 140 million people, and it's almost double the size of Ireland, so Ireland looked completely empty in my head. I was flying for nearly sixteen hours. I was very, very tired, so I slept for nearly twenty hours. Then when I woke up, it was a nice autumn day, so I went out of the house to look around. It looked very quiet, and not so many people, but friendly people said, 'Hi, hello.' I went for a walk around the Lough, I saw the swans, it was very enjoyable.

After two days, I had my first lecture, so I came to my institute and I met the people there. I found that people were very friendly. I remember one of the guys, he asked me to go for a drink, and I said, 'I don't drink,' but then he said, 'It's OK, you may not drink, but you're always welcome.' So I went with them to the pub – it was Costigan's, very close to work – I saw that there were more people inside the pub than in the street, that was a bit surprising, but now I'm used to this. One guy, he got completely drunk, we had to carry him home. I see him almost every day now; he is a good friend of mine.

The Beamish pipeline

There is an Indian guy here who used to study with me, now he is working in Finland in Nokia. He showed me the Beamish brewery, and he said that from this brewery they sell the drinks to all the pubs in Cork by tap, you know they have a pipeline, like the way the water is transferred. I believed him.

I found that Cork is very similar to my home town in that sense – back home we always like to gather together in the evening, mainly in the tea shops; in Cork this has been replaced by the pubs, OK, but back home in Gachha every evening if I go home I

Above: The Berwick Fountain on the Grand Parade.
Below: A swan on the Lough.

Mahbub at the start of the 'pipeline.'

meet with all my friends in a tea shop, they always go there, my friends they'll find me more times in the tea shop than in my home.

I'm living here for six years you know, so it's more or less my second hometown, I really love it. And whenever I go outside of Cork you know, when I'm coming back I really feel that I am coming to my home. When I first came here, I came to a country where I didn't know anyone, but now I have met quite a few good friends, you know, and I have a good life, both in terms of my sports life, my work life, so I'm happy about all these things. In Ireland among all the accents, I love the Cork accent, because first of all I can understand it very well: people they all say I have a little bit of it, which I am proud of.

Robert Fourie
[When I came here first] I found a little flat in Skiddy's Alms House, which is on the Northside there behind St. Anne's Church of Ireland church, the Shandon Bells really. My flat was looking out over that graveyard there behind St. Anne's Church, and kids from the Northside used to have cider parties outside my window. It was quite noisy at times, but the thing that really made a lot of noise was the St. Anne's bells that used to ring. They had the tourists going up there and ringing songs [on the bells] and, goodness gracious, you'd be asleep and be woken up by that all the time. And of course, those bells ring every fifteen minutes right through the night, it never stops. In the corner apartment I was directly opposite those bells. When I think of Cork I do think of the Shandon bells.

Shandon.

I remember when I first arrived in Cork, I remember standing on North Main Street and hearing a conversation between two older Cork people. One old lady was walking along, and she saw another old lady coming in the opposite direction, outside that church on North Main Street, it's got a green Byzantine dome on top of it. And the one said to her, 'Where are you off to girl?,' and the other one says, 'I'm off to Mass.' So the first one says, 'Would you ever say a prayer for me, so?' and the other one says 'Say your own feckin' prayer yourself.'

Dearbhla Kelleher
My father grew up in Sheares Street in Cork, the heart of town, and he's got some great stories all right. They'd be getting up to no good … from across the road from another person's window, they used to put black string across on the knocker on the other persons door across the road and they used to be knocking, and the people used to be coming out. They used get away with murder, I'd say. They'd hang around by the Mardyke, the Lee Fields and the baths. There used to be a dog named Rory and ever time the dog jumped in to the baths after them they'd get kicked out, and they always managed to wangle their way back again.

Geoffrey D'Souza

You might laugh at this, but I come from a sunny country, and a bit of the sun is always fantastic to see. There is a park by the shaky bridge, Fitzgerald's Park, and it's very near UCC, and it's a bit out of town. In summer I love going there and just sitting under the tree, reading a newspaper and just having warm sun. I don't long to go to a warm climate, because I come from there, so you know a winter climate is fantastic with me: I actually love it, as long as it's not raining on my head.

As an outsider that the pace of life is very interesting because it's a very relaxed and a slow pace of life, in a very nice and a positive sort of way. Your workplace is very near, you can be very close and you can be very comfortable, in that closed sort of circle. Like, back in Delhi you might have to travel an hour in a train to go to your job, and you know the whole city is so polluted, and there is just so much happening, and people are whizzing past you, you know. Over here, even on a road [in cars] you will see people are nice and polite.

Kay O'Carroll

You wouldn't go into town now very often, Saturday would be the day for town. There was Woolworth's in Patrick Street, and nearly everybody's treat was the ice cream cone in Woolworth's. You might have to queue for fifteen minutes like to get your cone, but once you got your cone you were happy, you didn't look for anything else.

People went to the local shops every day because they just got the milk for today, and the butter and the cheese; there were no fridges. Every Christmas if you were dealing in the local shop you got a candle and a lovely little fruit cake, just out of gratitude I suppose for giving your business for the year, but it was lovely. We had a local shop up to about three years ago, at the end of our road and it was fantastic . . . it was a lovely little shop … you might go to make a cup of tea, and you might be low in tea, and when you went in there you'd be chatting to the girl behind the counter. But while you were chatting somebody else would come in, and she'd get stuck in the conversation, and there could be four or five in the shop, like. And I often went down for a bar of chocolate, and I'd spend an hour down there and it would shorten the night, pass away the night. It's not like that in the supermarket: you go in and pick what you want, pay for it, and just run out the door. It was an awful loss, we all missed it terribly.

Our famous landmark you could say would be Shandon. Now, I spent most of my childhood down around there because my aunts came from near Shandon, and I never went to the top of Shandon until a few years ago. A person came from America, and we climbed the steps of Shandon and she played the bells, we didn't see much because it was a misty day. But there was a time when you couldn't go inside of Shandon, because it would be considered a sin, you know; it wasn't of your religion, like. So Shandon would be a landmark that you would only just take for granted, really; you'd pass it down and you'd pass it up, and you'd only look up to see the time. The North Cathedral would be another, well that was where we were all christened, and where we all made our Communion, and all our parents and grandparents were all married there.

Talking about meeting places now, years ago there was Singer's [Corner], people would say, if they had dates now or if they were meeting friends, 'I'll meet you at Singer's.' The

Singer's Corner.

Savoy was another meeting place – the steps of the Savoy – that was a cinema, there was a beautiful restaurant upstairs. You went into the back of the cinema – you'd have to go up about maybe a hundred steps – that's because it was cheap, if you went in the front way it was dearer. You used to go into the back and you'd be breathless when you'd get to the top, and it would be packed.

I love down around Oliver Plunkett Street, isn't it funny? I'd favour that now more than Patrick Street, and I mean the main street now is all pedestrianised and looking totally different. They're all objecting to the lights, you'd think the lights were going to fall down on top of you and kill you, you know, they're not straight up poles with lights anymore. Now I just love to go down around Oliver Plunkett Street, there is kind of a warmth or something there. And the North Main Street is lovely then because you go through and you meet lots of people that you know because everybody from the Northside takes their route through the North Main Street.

Change

People aren't as close: years ago everybody lived near everybody, so they saw people on a daily basis, but now so many people have kind of moved out into the suburbs, and people mightn't see each other, unless they get into their car and drive the ten or fifteen miles to meet up. When I was growing up, you had Cork city and the country: Blarney was the country, Ballincollig was the country. You never went there because it was like another

Oliver Plunkett Street.

area: to us it would have been nearly another country. Blarney and Ballincollig and places like that, they're an extension of the city now.

Karina Abdoulbaneeva

Best thing about Cork city? I like that it's small because I can take just two steps and get everything I need. I can go to chemist, and to the supermarket straight away, and to the bank, or to the post office, and everything is so close; you don't really need to spend much time. In Cork, when you come to the city centre you need half an hour to do many things, and that's very different from my country because you have to spend many hours, especially if you are living in Moscow. You have to go by the tube, and you need to spend two hours just to get from some shop to some bank, so that's what I really like, it's very convenient and so homely.

Andy Hawkins

When I walk into a bar, and this is another aspect of being home [from abroad], I'll know most of the people sitting around the bar and I can have a chat … I could have a great social night just meeting an old friend and chatting at the bar. Whereas when I was abroad — when I was living in New Zealand, Australia, in America — I could go into a bar and know absolutely no-one. It can be very lonely in a big city. And they've got this thing here, 'ballhopping.' I absolutely love that. They come in and they'll say something to you, and it will be something totally outrageous, like, but of course … they're only larking, they're only slagging you, right? But of course, if you are gullible – and people are – they'll believe it and, of course, there's always a couple in the crew that know it's a 'ballhop' except you … until the penny drops, you know? Now, ballhopping I think is uniquely Irish … I think it's just a Cork thing.

Another thing is; you're walking down Shandon Street, you might meet Joe on the street:

'Joe, where are you going?'

'I'm going up along, well, where are you going?'

'I'm going down along' and

'Later on I'll meet you out along.'

That's totally a Cork thing, right? All that sort of thing. That to me is great.

12

Alan Botan

I am Alan Botan from Kurdistan in Northern Iraq, and I am asylum seeker in Cork, for more than two years and four months. There are five thousand people in the area where I was born, the population is not so big. My family are living in Kurdistan. I have two brothers and two sisters, and my father and my mother. The situation became that I had to leave that country, and at the moment I am here. [At home] the neighbours they were lovely, I had a lovely time with them. I had a friend, we were always going to school together, and we played games together, then doing our homework and then going home and sleeping. The games that we played – we used to put seven stones, flat stones upon each other, and then we throw the ball at the stone and when the stone is falling down you have to run away, because if the others catch the ball, and they will throw it at you and if they catch you, you have lost the game. As a group you can play three on one side and three on the other, or four on one side and four on the other.

My favourite meal in Kurdistan is *Dolma*, that is made of vegetables and rice inside, all sorts of vegetables and rice, and meat - chicken or lamb or cow – in the pot and then cook it slowly and it is very lovely. I always asked my Mum to cook that as a special meal at the weekend. My childhood: going to school and coming back, and going to the shop if there is shopping for Mum. We had a little farm, we used to go with Mum and Dad, doing the farming and helping them.

To be honest, my first day when they sent me to school, my Mum sent me by force because I was so scared of the teacher. So they took me to school, and then I ran away and came back home. My Mum, again she sent me back there, she took my hand and she sent me back there, and I settled down and I made a friend and I stayed with him.

My grandmother is still alive. My grandmother is very, very kind. Sometime, when I didn't have money when I was child, she put her hand in her pocket, and she give me money to spend for sweets. Always she protects as a grandmother, and she is really a good grandmother. She lives with my parents, because in our culture we have to protect our old. My grandma at the moment she is very old, she is more than one hundred years. Once, my brother took her to my uncle's house, fifteen minutes by car, she always wants to meet my other uncle and to visit all the children and then come back home. My brother took her to my uncle just for one hour, and she said, 'Oh my God, I miss my family so much, I miss my other family [Alan's parents] and you have to return me back to my family.' So they returned back there, and after one hour she said, 'Oh my God, I haven't

seen my other son for more than three years and I have to go there.' And my father and
my brother took her again to my uncle's house, and in the end it was bring and back,
bring and back, many times, and there was a soldier on the way, at a checkpoint, and he
said, 'What are you doing with this woman? We can see you are bringing her here and
returning there, what's going on?'

[I arrived in Cork in] December 2002. To be honest the Cork accent is very fast; if you
ask any stranger, they are speaking so fast. Once when I was in the class, the teacher ask
me, 'How's the Cork accent?' And I said, 'To be honest I'm like a parrot, I can't understand
anything.' When I came my language wasn't good, and many [were saying to me], 'Do you
know what I mean?' in this kind of accent, and I said, 'No.' I didn't understand it first of
all. It was funny, and they made fun sometime and they laughed at me. The nicest one, it
was when I was out with my friends, and they were asking me, 'How's the craic, how's
the craic boy?' And I just stopped and I couldn't answer anything. I said, 'Michael, could
you please tell me what does it mean?' He was just laughing at me and said, 'It's nothing,
come on boy, it's nothing. [It means] how's your night?'

First of all when I came here I found it a little bit hard to integrate with the people,
because you are alone and a stranger, and I found it hard for more than six months, until
I improved my English and then I integrated with the people. I found many different
people from other countries – Spanish, or Italian – and we made a group, and for me
that's a circle of happiness, because I was a stranger and I came and I found some other
people. And I went between [among] the people: I knew them and I know them, and
they became friendly for me … and I love Cork.

To be honest the thing that I didn't like so much was drunk people, a lot of drunk
people at the night [in Cork], and I saw them and it wasn't so nice, but it's habit, and you

Out and about.

On the birthday trip.

cannot do anything. I can accept that because there are many countries they have the same situation. They make me a little bit concerned and afraid to be honest, about myself: I am far away from home, and a stranger here, but things will get better I think.

The most beautiful [surprise was] when it was 2003, my friends for my birthday took me to Galway and the islands. It was remarkable, I'll never forget. We started from Cork, then went to Killarney, the Ring of Kerry, the Gap of Dungloe, Lady's View, Dingle; then we took a ferry and saw Fungi the dolphin. Then we moved to the Galway, and then the Aran Islands, I spent two days there, it was fabulous: sunshine and a lot of landscape, and I cycled.

There isn't really a Kurdish community in Cork, but we have here more than twenty people, all Kurdish from different regions. For the New Year, our New Year, 21st of March, the same day that the spring is coming, we join together and we go to the pub, for drinking and dancing and celebration. Our New Year they call Navruz.

Favourite places
There's a lovely park on the river of Lee, just over near what they call Victoria Road. And sometimes in the evening, when the sun shines, you go there and sit beside the river – it's lovely I think. And the second place is for me UCC – I love UCC so much, the architecture in the buildings is lovely, and also [I like it] because you can see more different people there, foreigners, and for me it's much nicer. All the people you can see there, I enjoy it so much.

13

Mícheál Ó Geallabháin

I was born in South Terrace, one of the post-war children, but I grew up in Carroll Street, which is right across the road from the Bridewell barracks, down at the bottom of Cornmarket street or the Coal Quay. I grew up in that general area of the North Main Street, Carrolls Quay, Cornmarket Street, Corporation buildings. The Coal Quay was very active at the time, and it was excitement to go up and see what was going on. One of the earliest memories I have of living there is waking up in the morning time two or three times a week to hear the farmers coming in from Whitechurch, and Carrignavar and wherever, you know and there would be vegetables and you would hear donkeys braying, and you'd go up to Simcox' to buy some bread in the bakery, you'd see lovely apples and carrots and spuds.

Cars you didn't come across too often. At night-time you'd never hear cars, it was dead silent. And you would hear people going home, especially at the weekend, from the pubs down town, and some of them would be drunk going up towards the North Gate Bridge, going back up home, and some of them you would recognise, and you'd say, 'Oh, there's Nancy, she's going home, she's drunk again,' but it was a very safe environment, an atmosphere of total safety and security.

When I was a kid lighting in the house was by gas; we'd always wait 'till my father came home from work at Beamish brewery, and it was almost like a ceremony. He would get up on a stair, and strike a match and light the gas. It was poor lighting but we thought it was great, and then electricity came in the mid 50s. Monday was the day the women did all the washing, and everybody had to dry the clothes out the back, and if it was raining it was hassle for the women because they couldn't get the clothes dried. Nobody had any cars. I remember going to a wedding in 1951 or thereabouts, down the Metropole, my aunt Mary got married, and there was high excitement going down in a big car. Going in a car was a strange thing, and being dressed up and seeing everybody else dressed up, and being treated as a Lord down there at the age of five or six.

The shops that were there, the dealing women would have second hand clothes, because people didn't have the money to buy new ones. And I remember being sent up by my mother – I was eight years of age – up to the North Main Street to buy something in Conor Farrell's grocery shop, and I went up Carroll Street past the Bridewell, up Kyle Street. And then on the way back some of the dealing women who had clothes shops on Kyle Street said, 'Little boy, come over here, boy.' And I was seven or eight, and I wondered,

Mícheál age 10 in 1955, practising for the Flageolet Band in his school on Sullivan's Quay.

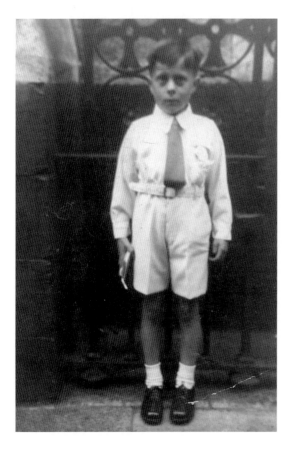

Mícheál on his First Communion day in 1952, outside St. Peter and Paul's.

Mícheál in UCC, where he is a doctoral candidate.

'What do they want?' 'Boy, that's a lovely pants and jacket you have on, who made that for you?' And I said, 'Me Mam,' and the women looked at each other knowingly; 'Oh yeah, she's the one who can make the clothes.' 'All right, boy, go on away now.' These are the things still fresh in my mind now, you know.

One of my earliest memories was 1954 with my father. I was nine years of age, and my father took myself and my brother Jerry down to Patrick Street to see the Cork team coming in. And there was Christy Ring, 'Oh my God, Christy Ring,' standing on a double-decker bus, holding the Liam McCarthy cup. I thought Cork would never possibly ever lose a match, it was going to go on forever and ever, winning all the time.

We were all short of money, but the mothers felt that education was the way out of the poverty trap, and it certainly was. And the women way back in those days, my mother and all the other mothers, they sacrificed themselves, because they were clever people, they were intelligent people, but they didn't get the chance, but by goodness they were going to give their children a chance. One of the negative sides of the fifties was everybody emigrating, you know and I remember when I was going to Sullivan's Quay school and [the teacher said], 'Murphy, where's your book?' 'Sir, we're all going to England, in a couple of weeks time, so Mam and Dad said there's no point in getting books because we won't be here.' And the whole family, parents and all the children, just everybody out. And I could see no end to it, this was going to go on forever, people were going to be emigrating forever, things would never get better. And everybody was coming back from England, during the summer holidays, who had gone over there to work: they all had nice suits on, they were able to buy the Examiner every day, and there was real money, and that sense of what you did not have, was almost as important as what you did have going for you.

I used to love the old part, North Main Street, South Main Street, I used to love the more intimate streets: Oliver Plunkett Street, Princes Street, Maylor Street. I suppose what to me is the most important thing of all is that my family are here, this is where I belong, this is where I grew up. Since I came back to live in Cork in 2001, I met a lot of people that I hadn't seen for thirty or forty years, you're fitting back into what is really your territory you know, and I suppose to me Cork is where I grew up, it's where I belong, it's where my people are.

A joke
One of my sisters was out there in Spain a couple of years ago, and there was slagging going on between the Dublin and Cork crowd. It was 'Even Stevens' until one of the Cork people said to the Dublin crowd: 'How would you recognise a Corkman with an inferiority complex?'

And they said, 'We don't know.'

He said, 'He's a fella who thinks he's the same as everybody else.'

14

Parting Words

In the interviews, we asked many of the contributors the following two questions.
'What message would you have for the people of Cork?'
'When I say, "Cork city," what (three) words come to mind?'
Many of us would find these questions hard to answer 'off-the-cuff', and many might give different answers on different days. However, here are some of the sentiments and images that came as a response: parting words.

Tim O'Brien

People used to talk about 'the old Blackpool' and 'the old Fairhill,' and all this kind of thing; that there was great communities in those areas. And there might have been, but unfortunately now is now, then is then, and you have to look to the future to see what is going to be there. And there is good hope like; the people of Cork are always very solid. It doesn't matter what happens to them; they nearly always kind of surface. When people didn't have a lot, they got on with what they had to do, and they made sport for themselves. So if they get back to the idea of having a bit of a laugh again, as against trying to make a financial success of everything, I'd say the people would probably be a lot better off.

Geoffrey D'Souza

I'd just like to say, you know like, it's been a nice time, and I never regretted coming here. When I was coming to Cork, a lot of people were telling me, 'You're crazy,' maybe they thought I was making a mistake. Cork grew up as well, you know, with so many Europeans coming in, like. We used to have a lot of problem staffing people, but now we have a lot of Slovenians, Slovakians, Georgians, and catering has become a lot more multi-cultural and it's a lot easier. In my way I can see this small city growing up in a very, very positive way as well, it's becoming more global and it's more mellow, and, and it's more upbeat, you know: you see a bit of colour, you see a bit of Chinese, you see Italians, you see Indians, they're all doing their thing, and they all blend in, which is fantastic.

Aimée Setter

Be kind to your neighbour, don't always judge a book by its cover, get to know people, and put your rubbish in the bin.

Tim in Anglesea Street Fire
Brigade Station where he
works.

B. O'D.
A message to the people of Cork … thanks very much for accepting me, and I'm still
here. I hope it's going to stay the way it is, it's not going to go too crazy, that it's going to
keep the Irish bit to it: that's the message for Cork.

Robert Fourie
A lot more African people have come to Cork – you see a lot more African faces on the
streets. Around UCC campus there's a lot of Muslim girls and a lot of Muslim guys, doing
medical courses, and there are a number of Chinese people and a lot of Nigerians, and
people from Africa, some of them refugees, some of them not, but you don't see people
talking to each other, and I think that's a problem, I don't get a sense that people are
talking to each other. There are going to be more and more foreign faces in Ireland and
Cork particularly, but unless those cultures are given some way of fitting in, I think that
could lead to a dangerous situation where people start hating each other. I mean coming
from South Africa I'm particularly aware of that, that kind of racial division can cause
havoc, and I think something active needs to be done about getting people to talk to each
other, and to realise that we're human, we're similar.

   People possibly don't realise how nice it is to go to bed and not have to worry that
somebody's going to break into your house and murder you while you are in your bed,
which a lot of people in other countries have to deal with. South Africa particularly,
whether you are white or black, you are going to suffer under crime at some point. I have
been mugged myself, I have had my car broken into while I was still driving, and I've had
a house been broken into while I was in the house, and I have no doubt that if they got
into the house and the dogs hadn't frightened them away, that I might not be here today.

I think Irish people don't realise how safe they are, and how lucky they are, to live in an environment where guns are not so … on average you are safe in Ireland – you don't have to worry about being murdered and being hurt in general.

Karina Abdoulbaneeva

Cork is so different now, and I see the changes in the attitude of people as well, because so many foreign people came to Ireland. I think Irish people are changing, because when I was here seven years ago I was probably just one foreign girl, I never met any other foreigners around me. Everybody was Irish, and everybody was so interested; 'Where [do] you come from, and what are you doing here, and what brought you to Ireland?' And now I see so many foreign people, and Irish people probably become more relaxed, more open, and what I like [is that] they accept people, they accept different cultures. I understand that it's probably not easy because in Ireland you always were closed, but now I see changes in the mind of Irish people, and changes in their attitude.

I'm really grateful to many people I met here in this city, and I'm really grateful to Cork because this city, and of course the people who are living here, gave me so many opportunities to realise my ideas. I feel that I can make many things, much more than I could do in another country. And I realised myself here, and my dreams in this city became true. I see how I realised my dreams, and I'm really, really grateful to people who helped me here. I know this is not an easy time for me, the first years are always difficult, but I think I made so many important things for myself in this city, and I think it's just because I had so many helpful people around. What I want to say is 'thank you' to people who helped me a lot, and there are loads of people who did that, and I want to say I love them.

Stefan Wulff

A message for the people of Cork? Well, I suppose: remember who you are. There are lovely idiosyncrasies in the Cork people, people are nice, people are welcoming, and keep it up that way, and be more open and keep being open, to people who may come from a different background, who mightn't be familiar with what's happening here, and people in Cork mightn't be familiar with what's happening for them, and try to make the best of things as they occur.

Avreimi Rot

People here are a bit not aware of what's happening in the world, it's kind of an enclosed environment, the only information that people get is from the media, which is really one-sided. I would like people to be more modest about their opinions. Not being opinionated about what's happening around them in the world because things are complicated. Well, it's obvious for me when I say I'm from Israel it arises many questions about the situation. It's the first thing that I encounter with, but these are the things; because not having too much of politics here in Cork, which is south of Ireland and there was not too many things in politics around here so it's more like a game for most of the people. I'm not talking about Israel but any kind of things that are happening in the world, that they are not aware of the complexity . . .

Stefan with some Noamhóga Chorcaí currachs.

I guess in a way, just like maybe taking things more seriously, appreciating this amazing and quiet place in the world which is, like, a fertile land for art and for culture and lot of music, and people do enjoy it, and still knowing that there is a world around and things happening in the world, and there are wars somewhere and there are famines in other places, and things are serious and they are happening while here is quiet and calm . . . Maybe what should change is the awareness of people of the seriousness and complexity of other things happening in the world.

Andy Hawkins
Now, when I came home to Ireland I was already used to living in what I would describe as a multicultural society. As you can imagine, they are from all over the world in Australia, but I wasn't prepared for that in Ireland. My son once said to me the reason he wouldn't live in Ireland was that he couldn't get over the fact that everyone was Irish. It took my son to point that out to me. And I said, 'Well, what's the problem?' He says 'Well, back in Australia I've Greeks, Vietnamese, Italians, Germans in the classroom.' I don't think the people in Cork were prepared for this onslaught of multiculturalism. And I had to resign myself to the fact that nothing stays the same, but Cork, or Ireland, didn't change, it just jumped. It jumped ahead, like.

You talk to twenty-year-olds, they're spending a fortune in drink and all that sort of thing and they've got this very sort of slack attitude – 'The country owes us something.' I think they should go abroad. I know for a fact that if they spend a couple of years, they're going to come back a different person. They're going to pick up things, obviously. So from

Andy in Plymouth,
England, in 1973.

that point of view, I was happy and sad about Ireland, to be honest with you. I was happy that people had the things like, people were getting houses, but I also thought when I was growing up here there wasn't many jobs, [but] community spirit was there, and I think that's gone. The young people have money now, you see, and they're just spending it and spending it; they're going out, they want the latest car, they want the latest this, the latest that. Even adults. They're not contented to live in the house they got married in, they're 'upgrading.' This is the term I'm hearing now, 'upgrading' … rather than being contented with what they have. Now that to me is a form of greed, which I never saw in the Irish people as I was growing up.

What I'd say to the people who are listening to this [interview] is that you'll have to be tolerant of the 'New Irish.' I don't call them non-nationals at all, I do not like that term. I call them the 'New Irish' because one day, one of these 'New Irish' might end up being a politician, a famous musician, a footballer, whatever, so let's accept them. I know you'll take the good with the bad as I found out when I was abroad myself, but I'm back home in Ireland now and we should give these people a chance, give the 'New Irish' a go in this country and we will actually benefit down the line from it. In fact, I think we benefit from them already, like in the fact that you go in town here and you'll see the Russian shop, you'll see the African food shop, you know? All these things. And they will mix with us. You must remember they're kind of feeling us out as we're feeling them out, but eventually the melting pot will work, and that will take years. It won't take five minutes or five months, it will take years, but it will work.

Kay on a visit to England in 1995.

Kay O'Carroll

Do I have any message for the people of Cork? I suppose just maybe to stay as nice, you know, stay as nice as they are. The people of Cork are really lovely: you'll always feel safe like, if you're down town and you faint on the footpath, like, you'll be looked after, you know you'd be put into an ambulance, and somebody would hop in and go with you. The people of Cork, I wouldn't change them for the world.

Cork in three words

Adam Skotarczak

Nice and friendly people, a lot of colours, different colours in the city, and I think traffic jams. Yes it's true.

B. O'D.

Small city, friendly people and the Cork accent, that's the three words.

Liz Steiner-Scott

I don't know if I could do it in three words. Can I do it in more than three words? I love Cork and I think Cork has this amazing spirit. You only had to see it with the Hurling Final [2004 all-Ireland hurling final between Cork and Kilkenny] you know on Sunday, and that feeling that it really is still very tribal. I think that there is that sense that Cork people relate to each other in that way, and that's lovely. On the other hand there is an element in Cork where I think it is very much a second city in the country - they resent Dublin as being the capital city, and because everything happens in Dublin, there is a sense in which Cork people, I think we all feel slightly annoyed that everything is in Dublin. I know I do: if I go to meetings and they're always in Dublin, and you always think, 'God, why do I have to keep going to Dublin, why don't the Dublin people come down here?' But that is very much a second city experience. When I first came to Cork, when [the Irish Examiner] was still the Cork Examiner, 'the paper' you know, there was a sense in which those of us who still read the Irish Times we were not really Cork people. So there is that sense, I think that Cork is tribal, and it's got great spirit, but it suffers a little bit for feeling that it is the second city.

I think that Cork has been physically transformed so much. The other night when the team came back down, they came down Patrick Street. The new Patrick Street is beautiful, and I know we were all very cynical about it, but I was looking at it on camera, thinking, 'It really is beautiful now.' And I don't usually say that about Cork. I have to say I don't see Cork as being beautiful, but it does look really lovely now, so I have to kind of revise my feeling towards Cork because I think Cork is looking quite nice these days. When they finally finish digging it up it will be nice.

Stefan Wulff
Lee, chaos, change.
The Lee always kind of stuck out as a river flowing through a city and adding so much more flair to it. I suppose that might be debatable as regards to everything that goes into it, which one mightn't want to think about too closely, but coming into Cork city, Patrick's Bridge, it really does something for me.

Now chaos, I suppose it's the traffic I'm referring to. I would have cycled for the first couple of years all over the place, which was a great way of transport and I was grateful for having the bike. Obviously the whole infrastructure in Cork was geared towards small [numbers of] cars, but the whole thing evolved, traffic grew, there are more and more cars on the streets, and just congestion all over the place. And on top of that, typical Irish, or particularly Corkonian behaviour, to park everywhere you want, it doesn't matter if you block the road, you already have a car parked on one side of the road, it doesn't matter if you park on the other side of the road, and nobody else can get through. So that to some extent amused me, to another extent annoyed me, and I suppose I would have been used to cycling in a haphazard way myself, so it would have suited me down to the ground.

The change that took place particularly over the past five years I think is just phenomenal. I'm saying that in a very neutral way, so I'm not sure if that is a good thing or a bad thing; I suppose it's both. Remembering coming to Cork and getting around in Cork ten years ago, there were certain areas where I thought, 'This is unbelievable,' this reminded me of the years after rebuilding Germany, and you would have had really very poor architecture, very neglected areas. One area that sticks in my mind would be the North Mall: that would have been extremely grey, a lot of dilapidated houses, and at the same time there was a nice flair in that area but really on a bad day it really could have an impact on somebody's mood, like, and certainly the Coal Quay similarly.

I think [change] is probably a nationwide thing now, people seem to have less time. The economy is a big issue here and it seems to have been a very positive issue from a numerical point of view; people have jobs in the first place, they have good incomes, the banks are throwing money at people so most people can afford to buy houses. The social housing sector has changed, luckily, and was very badly needed, and it's not finished. So that's a positive thing; but at the same time I think people really exposed a certain greediness, and I think it has spread onto more and more people. The shopping centres get bigger and bigger, and sometimes I feel everything has got to do with consumerism. I really regret that. And you know, in a way, I have noticed that if you look at certain characters on the streets of Cork, they seem to have, I won't say evaporated, they have not completely gone, but there are fewer and fewer of those people to be found, because there are fewer and fewer places for them to go. Certain pubs that would have been quirky and manky, but at the same time they would have been the attraction for people to come in to talk and just take your time; now you have the bleeding superpubs, and all this kind of superficial ding-dong, so that's a sad thing to realise.

Lode Vermeulen
It is different in a good way, it has atmosphere, it has its own attitude. That's what I like here in Ireland; people have respect for each other, there is social security for people, people are always willing to help each other, and people don't mind if you have a big car or a small car. That's what I really love here in Ireland: 'It's your life so do what you want,' but if you need help people are always willing to help you, that's really great.

Michael O'Flynn
I just love Cork, and I wouldn't want to be anywhere else bar Cork. 'Tis my roots, 'tis my home, 'tis my love.